THE

LUCIFER
FILES

THE
LUCIFER
FILES

KEN McFARLAND

Pacific Press Publishing Association
Boise, Idaho
Oshawa, Ontario, Canada

Edited by Lincoln E. Steed
Designed by Tim Larson
Cover photo by Duane Tank
Type set in 10/12 Century Schoolbook

Unless otherwise indicated, scripture references in this book are from the New International Version.

The author assumes full responsibilty for the accuracy of all facts and quotations cited in this book.

Library of Congress Catalog Card Number: 88-80973

ISBN 0-8361-0775-X

88 89 90 91 92 • 5 4 3 2 1

Contents

1. The Sword of Damocles 9
2. Invasion of a Supervirus 15
3. Battlezone Earth 23
4. Two Words 30
5. Newton's Third Law 37
6. The Late Average Joe 47
7. Echoes of Eden 55
8. The War Behind All Wars 64
9. Whodunit? 75
10. Duel in the Desert 83
11. Duel on the Mountain 93
12. Confessions of a News Junkie 102
13. Why the War Isn't Over 113
14. The End—The Beginning 122

A Word From the Author—

As a means of communicating spiritual truth, the allegory has always served an honored and important place in religious literature. Bunyan's *Pilgrim's Progress* and *The Screwtape Letters* by C. S. Lewis are well-known examples of this genre.

While most of this book is based squarely on what the Bible tells us about the great war between Christ and Satan, the "Lucifer Files" themselves are allegorical. Yet even these "files" are not simply pure fiction—the result of unfettered imagination. They are based fully on what is known from Inspiration of the fallen angel's goals, thoughts, and plans.

Some may question the propriety of "giving the devil his due," as it were, even in the title of this book. In considering the great controversy now raging, most of us who are aware of it at all most often think of it from God's perspective. We want, understandably, to identify with the ultimate winner of the contest.

Yet, one of the first great rules of any battle is "Know thine enemy." This book attempts to expose the driving motives, the calculated plans, and the innermost thoughts and feelings of our great common enemy. Those who read this book through will realize, however, that in exposing Satan, these pages in no way invest him with any qualities other than those of the true supervillain that he is. The real hero of this book—it will be plainly seen—is Jesus Christ, the most magnificent personality of all history.

It is my conviction that all of us would profit immensely as we realize how starkly real are the characters, places, and events involved in this titanic struggle between good and evil. This world is altogether too present and real to us. If *The Lucifer Files* helps to heighten the reality of the unseen war behind all wars, it will have more than fulfilled its intended purpose.

Ken McFarland
March 1988

Chapter 1
The Sword of Damocles

When you're really good at something, nothing beats getting paid to do it. And Damocles was very, very good at what he did.

He had hired on as a courtier to the tyrant Dionysius, who ruled Syracuse in Sicily in the fourth century B.C. Then, as now, being a tyrant was not all fun and games. In fact, running a dictatorship could be a real headache.

But no self-respecting tyrant would ever be caught without a courtful of jolly types whose job it was to take his mind off his troubles and make him feel good about things.

Through comedy, drama, optimism, and flattery, these entertainers were charged with keeping the royal mood sunny side up. Show biz for an audience of one.

And nobody was better at the job than Damocles. He was the quintessential optimist, the ultimate positive thinker, the definitive master of flattery.

But apparently, in time a more realistic Dionysius began to weary of the relentlessly rose-colored view of life advanced by Damocles. His everlasting good cheer and obsequious fawning were beginning to get on the king's nerves.

Determined to make his point with Damocles,

legend has it that Dionysius invited him to a banquet. Once seated, Damocles looked up to find himself sitting directly under a sword suspended by a single thread.

The not-so-subtle message Dionysius intended Damocles to pick up on was that life is not all undiluted happiness and success. The threat of danger hangs over all of life's endeavors. Suspended over life's good is the constant menace of evil.

I can identify with Damocles.

Like him, I prefer to accentuate the positive. I'm attracted to upbeat, optimistic people, and I try to avoid gloomy pessimists who look for the dark lining on every silver cloud.

Life can be good and pleasant and happy. It brings to each of us its share of joys both small and great.

> Watching a baby's smile.
> Falling in love.
> Graduating with honors—or sometimes,
>   just graduating at all.
> Acing a college exam.
> Winning a promotion.
> Becoming a father or mother.
> Buying your dream house—or sometimes,
>   just being able to afford buying
>   a house at all.
> Watching your team win.
> Learning a new skill.

Yet, for all the good and beautiful and joyous that life holds—and for all the effort we may put forth to look on the bright side—a certain vague sadness and indefinite fear constantly haunts us.

Fear, because we are not safe. Fear of the crime,

disease, accidents, or disasters that can snatch us—or those we love—away at any moment. Fear that we may somehow lose our most prized possessions or relationships. And, in recent years, even the fear of possible nuclear annihilation.

Sadness, because no matter how good life gets, we know we're dying. Why does life have to be so short? We begin with high hopes and bright dreams, with energy and drive. But all too soon the accelerating years cruelly assault our bodies, minds, and plans, stealing away much of what makes life worthwhile. We've only just begun to live, it seems, when suddenly it is time to die.

The daily news forcibly reminds us that, for all the admitted good it may possess, our world is nonetheless blighted with an appalling burden of evil. Here where we live the tears never stop. The hospitals are never empty. The jails are always crowded. The nations are never at peace. Here, the daily news is of terrorism and scandal and divorce and starvation and child abuse and drug addiction and war and death.

Here on our planet, violence is entertainment and life is cheap. Decency and morality must fight to survive. Here on earth our lives are filled with fear and pain and worry and heartbreak as we march our weary way to the grave.

Our world is a vast colony of unspeakable misery, a seething caldron of personal and national violence, a whirling sphere in space without a single safe haven from the all-pervasive reach of selfishness.

It's as if good and evil are locked in desperate combat—as if two titanic forces somewhere in the universe are having it out to the death with Earth as the battlezone.

Is it possible that behind all the wars of Earth a

much greater war rages? Is it possible that every occurrence of earthly conflict—from a playground fistfight to a world war—is simply one skirmish in the ongoing war behind all wars?

Prepare now, in the pages just ahead, to break beyond the here and now. Prepare to stretch your mind to take in something bigger than anything you'll ever hear on the network news. Prepare to expand your focus to consider a reality so far-reaching that it staggers the imagination.

For in the pages that follow, the curtain will be drawn back to expose an enormous controversy between good and evil that many of us may never have dreamed existed. For, indeed, we are in the midst of a war that reaches back beyond human time—that reaches out from planet Earth to the entire cosmos.

And this battle is for real. This is no Star Wars/Star Trek science-fiction drama. But despite its stark reality, the world's media have chosen to deny and ignore it, reporting instead simply on its obvious effects. Which explains why so much of the evil reported by the media each day seems so random, so senseless.

It's the old problem of being unable to see the whole forest for concentrating on individual trees. Step back now—far enough to see the forest, to take in the big picture, to discover the "Why?" of evil by seeing it in its context.

Prepare yourself. For now we begin to open . . . THE LUCIFER FILES.

Database 5, File H-9073.811, Record 291
[Late 1980s]
Strategy Directive 11437.52
RE: Substrategy Reminders

I don't need to remind you, as my Central Imperial Staff, that in harmony with the Grand Strategy, it is to our benefit in some areas of the world to be direct and open in doing our work.

However, you also know that in many other areas, covert operations are more effective. Results from implementing the Secular Humanism Task Force substrategy are actually in advance of our estimates.

In those designated areas where the substrategy is in effect, Targets [human beings] must be led to believe that neither the enemy [God] nor I exist. This is vital.

The reality of a place called Heaven—of a real and personal god or devil—must be forcefully opposed. The book of lies [the Bible] must be presented either as irrelevant or as wholly human in origin. Its early history must be presented as legend or allegory. And any serious belief in the truth and reality of these things must be dismissed as hopelessly naive—as the sign of an unsophisticated, unenlightened, immature mind.

Keep our image benign—even humorous. Encourage the old stereotypes—the horns-and-pitchfork images. And keep the Targets busy making light of the book of lies and the existence of either god or devil.

Aggressively oppose any speech, book, or other communication you encounter that exposes the War and its agents as real. In the designated areas, we simply must stay under cover. As usual, pass this directive on to your subordinates.

Lucifer,
Commander-in-chief, Imperial Forces
King of Earth
Most High God in Exile
UNIVERSAL EMPIRE

Special note to the reader:

A brief explanation here on the organization of the Lucifer Files may prove helpful. The files contain five databases containing entries from the following time periods:

Database 1	From Lucifer's creation to the entrance of sin
Database 2	The war in Heaven
Database 3	From the creation of man to the birth of Christ
Database 4	The period of Christ's life on earth
Database 5	From the time of Christ to the present

This book will contain only a small sampling from the Lucifer Files. Selections will be of three types:

1. Imperial orders
2. Strategy directives
3. Journal entries

The first two file categories are directed to Lucifer's top level of command—the Central Imperial Staff. The third category, "journal entries," is Lucifer's personal record of events and of his own thoughts and feelings.

As written, the files contained an abundance of expletives which have been deleted in the abstracts appearing in this book.

Chapter 2
Invasion of a Supervirus

February 10, 1967.
Flatrock, Nevada.

Dr. Jeremy Stone stares in disbelief at the image on the electron microscope monitor. Here in this top-secret, five-level underground lab, he and his team have worked through the night to isolate the microbe, and they are running out of time.

Two days earlier, a classified military satellite named *Scoop VII*—after developing orbital instability—had been deliberately brought down in the Arizona desert. The two-man recovery team sent from Vandenberg Air Force Base had tracked the satellite's locator signal to the remote desert town of Piedmont, population 48.

Entering the village, the team reported that the streets were littered with bodies. At Vandenberg, where the progress of the recovery operation was being monitored by radio, the staff at Scoop Mission Control suddenly heard a high-pitched scream, followed by a crunching noise. Mission Control could not raise the two men again.

A second team, outfitted with air-tight suits and helmets, had then been dispatched to Piedmont. There they recovered the satellite and, to their surprise, found two survivors—an old man and an infant. The survivors and the satellite were then rushed to the underground Wildfire Lab just outside Flatrock, Nevada.

Searching for the cause of the mysterious deaths, the Wildfire team had discovered what they had feared might be true. The satellite had brought back from space a deadly extraterrestrial life form.

And now, their eyes riveted to the wall monitor, Dr. Stone and his colleagues watch the green crystalline microbe multiply rapidly. Unless they can find a way to neutralize it—and soon—it will quickly spread to destroy all life on earth.

So goes the chilling scenario of Michael Crichton's science-fiction best seller entitled *The Andromeda Strain*. When the book first appeared in January of 1969, it created no small stir. Six months later, when the real-life Apollo crew returned from the first manned lunar landing, the extensive quarantine measures implemented at the Lunar Receiving Lab were due at least in part to the low-grade "space bug" paranoia inspired by Crichton's thriller.

The Supervirus

Today we fear a possible space germ far less than we do a very real virus right here on Earth. HTLV-III/LAV—a killer virus that attacks the body's immune defense system—is the cause of AIDS, the most frightening epidemic to appear in hundreds of years. Once contracted, AIDS is 100 percent fatal and is a disease without a cure.

Our world has seen its share of epidemics. Between A.D. 1334 and 1351, up to 75 million people died in Eurasia of the plague known as The Black Death.

More soldiers died during the Civil War of typhoid fever than were killed in action. Another 20 million perished worldwide in 1918 and 1919 of influenza. Tens of millions more have died of cholera, smallpox, and other contagious diseases.

Yet the most lethal virus ever to devastate our planet is not AIDS or bubonic plague. This killer has proven far more horrific, and has swept away more millions, than any other epidemic in world history.

Realize it or not—believe it or not—every human being alive today is infected and is burdened daily with the appalling symptoms of this pandemic. This supervirus, to which all other diseases of Earth trace their origin, is SIN.

Sin is the ultimate cause of disease and death, of accidents, tragedies, and disasters. Grief and pain and violence and war and an endless host of other horrors exist solely as a result of the merciless invasion of the sin virus.

The urgent, haunting question is: Where did sin come from? And many explanations for the existence of evil in the world have been offered. Ancient legend volunteered that a curious Pandora unleashed evil on the world when she opened her sinister dowry box. Today we hear other answers.

Secular humanism theorizes that evil is normal— that is has been a natural part of human nature since the beginning of evolution. This theory has it that as man continues to evolve, he will steadily outgrow the evil in his nature and become more civilized. In this view of human nature, evil, and the universe, there is no room for the idea of a being called God.

Others believe that the universe was created by a Supreme Being, all right—but that He is an absentee landlord. God created everything, such maintain, and then walked off to leave human beings to make of their world and destiny whatever they should choose.

Still others say that God created people and the world perfect, but that something went terribly wrong—and that either God is not powerful enough to deal with the evil in the world or that He doesn't care enough to get involved.

The Origin of Evil

What is the truth? Where are the real answers?

Whatever your present beliefs, I want to challenge you—before you settle on your answers to life's truly big questions—to consider honestly the answers proposed by the world's all-time best seller—the Bible.

The Bible claims to be a message from God to us, in human language. It claims to have the only true answers to the *big* questions: Where did evil come from? Has it always been here? Will it ever end? Where did *I* come from? Why am I here? Where am I going?

The Bible takes us back to a time that may take real effort to imagine—a time when there was no sin, no trouble, no evil. It takes us back to a time long, long ago—to a place far, far away, A place called Heaven.

Here in Heaven is God's throne, from which He oversees the vast universe He has created. Countless angels—brilliant, intelligent, sinless beings whom He has also created—bask in the joy and love of His presence.

Reflecting His love of perfect order, each of the angels is assigned particular tasks. And the highest angel over them all is the one called Lucifer—"the shining one." Lucifer is the "covering cherub" and stands in the immediate presence of God.

"You were anointed as a guardian cherub," God said

of Lucifer, "for so I ordained you. You were on the holy mount of God; you walked among the fiery stones." Ezekiel 28:14. "You were the model of perfection, full of wisdom and perfect in beauty." Verse 12.

Database 1, File A-101.24, Record 77
Journal Entry 655.49

Today has been very pleasant and rewarding, Even more so, perhaps, than usual. At God's invitation, a number of us traveled at thought-speed to sector B/002 of quadrant 7 to watch Him finish creating an entire new galaxy.

The millions of us here at Headquarters continue to thank God for giving us life—and for filling our lives with so many challenges and pleasures. As for myself, I never cease to be humbled and honored that He has assigned to me such important responsibilities. Of all the billions of us He has created, why He chose me to stand at His side and to lead the others, I do not know. But it is my great joy and privilege to do His will.

I thank God that He created me with so many ways to enjoy the gift of life. I'm also thankful that He made all of us able to choose to worship Him—though any other choice is inconceivable. Why? Because we love Him without reservation. We trust Him without question. And we always will.

Lucifer,
Servant to the King

In perfect peace and sinlessness, the years of eternity past moved on. How long Lucifer had lived in Heaven since his creation the Bible does not tell us. Perhaps thousands of years. Perhaps millions.

But as time continued, Lucifer apparently became increasingly conscious of his own beauty and wisdom. And apparently he felt that he should be elevated to an even higher position in Heaven's line of authority.

Only two other beings in Heaven stood as equals with God the Father—Jesus Christ the Son, and the Holy Spirit. Lucifer, knowing God to be fair and truthful, doubtless concluded that God would soon recognize his personal growth, qualifications, and accomplishments and promote him to a position equal with that of the Son and the Spirit.

"Your heart became proud on account of your beauty, and you corrupted your wisdom because of your splendor." Verse 17.

"You corrupted your wisdom." In other words, Lucifer wasn't thinking straight. His judgment had become distorted by a false picture of himself that he had chosen to believe. Because of his wisdom, position, and beauty, Lucifer slowly came to see himself as more important in Heaven's scheme of things than he actually was. He had become *proud*. He had become *self-centered*.

Pride—an exaggerated sense of one's importance— sets one up for a fall. And fall Lucifer eventually did. After his fall, God would say of him, "You were blameless in your ways from the day you were created till wickedness was found in you." Verse 15.

"How you have fallen from heaven, O morning star, son of the dawn! . . . You said in your heart, 'I will ascend to heaven; I will raise my throne above the stars of God; I will sit enthroned on the mount of assembly, on the utmost heights of the sacred mountain. I will ascend above the tops of the clouds; I will make myself like the Most High.' " Isaiah 14:12-14.

Lucifer's promotion never came. If he had been

thinking clearly, he would never have lost sight of the fact that while God was the Creator, Lucifer was and could ever only be the creature. So he waited with increasing frustration in anticipation of something that could never happen.

As time passed with no indication that God was preparing for Lucifer's imminent elevation, the prince of the angels was at first puzzled, then bitterly disappointed—and finally, angered and jealous.

At this point, Lucifer could conclude only one of two things. Either the problem was with God—or it was with himself. Since the problem could not possibly be within himself, Lucifer reasoned, it had to be in God.

False Pictures of God

Despite all the apparent evidence to the contrary, Lucifer concluded, God was not fair, God was not just, God was not truthful. It seemed obvious to Lucifer that by affording special honors, privileges, and authority to Jesus, the Father was playing favorites. God simply must not be as He represented Himself to be to the universe. So the guardian cherub came sincerely to believe his own false ideas about God's character—fully accepting them as true.

For an extended period, Lucifer worked to convince the angels under him that the picture they had seen of God was inaccurate—that, in fact, He was a partial, unjust, unfair liar. Finally, the dissatisfaction Lucifer sowed ripened into a full-scale revolt.

"There was war in heaven, Michael [Christ] and his angels fought against the dragon [Lucifer], and the dragon and his angels fought back. But he was not strong enough, and they lost their place in heaven. The great dragon was hurled down—that ancient serpent called the devil or Satan, who leads the whole world astray. He was hurled to the earth, and his angels with him." Revelation 12:7-9.

Fully one third of the angels accepted and believed Lucifer's false picture of God and were thrown out of Heaven with him. See Revelation 12:3, 4.

The great battle between Christ and Lucifer—now called the devil or Satan—had begun. The supervirus of sin—of selfishness—had spread from Heaven to threaten Earth. And every funeral service and hospital ward, every day's burden of bad news from every point of the compass, remind us: The plague, the war, is REAL. It is here, now. Your choice aside, you are involved. You are affected.

Have you ever wondered if the virus has an antidote?

Have you ever wondered if the war will ever end?

Chapter 3
Battlezone Earth

Abraham Lincoln once received a rather unusual letter. Printed in large characters on the page was a single word: "Fool!"

Lincoln turned to an aide and said, "I have received a number of letters over the years from people who forgot to sign their names—but this is the first one I've ever received from someone who signed his name and forgot to write the letter!"

Just calling someone a fool doesn't make him one, of course. But Lincoln's critic was by no means the first to use the tactic of throwing mud in the hope that some of it would stick. We've already met the original mudslinger—the rebel angel Lucifer.

Determined to become equal with God, Lucifer in time convinced himself that God was a villain. And before being finally ejected from Heaven, he had also convinced a third of the angels that God was indeed an unfair tyrant.

Lucifer—"the shining one" had become Satan—"the accuser." The angel had become the devil. The covering cherub had become a malevolent mudslinger.

Evicted from Heaven, Satan and his fellow rebels set up the headquarters of their new counter-government on a small planet called Earth and pledged themselves

to everlasting hatred—and the ultimate destruction—
of their own Creator.

Database 3, File L-4101.293, Record 70
[Shortly following the creation of man]
Strategy Directive 406.93
RE: The New Race

Recently the enemy has created a new race—a new
form of supposedly intelligent life called human beings.
Indications are that the two prototypes will be capable of
reproducing themselves and that whatever duplicates
they reproduce will have the same capacity. The enemy
apparently hopes through this mechanism to populate all
of Earth.

Before any such duplication happens, it is vital that we
win the prototypes over to our cause. Success at this
would insure our undisputed control of this planet. It
would also strengthen our case in contending that the
obedience demanded by the enemy is not only arbitrary
but impossible. If it can be proven that human beings, in
addition to ourselves, are unable to live by the enemy's
code, then our cause will be vindicated.

Because the stakes are so high, I will personally lead
the effort to persuade the prototypes—known as Adam
and Eve—to see things as they are. As you undoubtedly
suspect, it will not be easy. Not only have they been
warned that we may approach them, but their eyes have
not yet been opened to reality.

Therefore they are as we once were, naively and
blindly trusting the enemy and powerfully influenced by
his so-called love. We, of course, know how seductive
the enemy's "love" can be. But now we know it for what
it is—sheer manipulation of others to gratify his ego and
to keep them in mindless subservience.

I have access to the humans at the tree in the center of Eden. I may temporarily be denied my rightful position in Heaven, but I retain my angelic powers—powers which for some unknown reason the enemy did not build into the new race.

I will exercise one of those powers to disguise myself as another life form. I have chosen the serpent. Tomorrow I will set the trap. Death to the enemy.

Lucifer,
Commander-in-chief, Imperial Forces
King of Earth
Most High God in Exile
UNIVERSAL EMPIRE

She hadn't intended to wander away from Adam. But somehow, happily preoccupied with her work, she suddenly found herself alone, looking up at the tree God had warned them about.

"You may eat the fruit from any tree in Eden," He had said. "But do not eat fruit from the tree in the center of the garden. If you do, you will most certainly die."

Now, as she looked curiously at the tree and noticed its attractive fruit, Eve wondered why God had declared this one tree off-limits.

"Did God really tell you not to eat fruit from any of the trees here in Eden?"

Startled, Eve searched for the source of the questioning voice. But all she could see was a serpent draped across the lower branches of the tree.

"I must say that you are breathtakingly beautiful," the voice continued. And now Eve could see that indeed the serpent was *talking*. Fascinating!

"Thank you," she replied. "But you are mistaken about the fruit. We are free to eat from any tree in the garden but this one. God says that if we eat fruit from this tree—or even if we touch it—we will die."

"You're kidding!" the serpent laughed. "Believe me, you *definitely* will *not* die! I've known God for a long time, and I can tell you that He was just trying to scare you. You see, He knows that the fruit of this tree has incredible power. Anyone who eats it moves up to a higher level of consciousness. In fact, those who eat this fruit will have the same knowledge and power that God has.

"Take me, for example. I'm just a serpent, but after eating this fruit, I'm able to speak, just as you can. And as you can see, I'm also very much alive!

"God doesn't want you and your husband to know what He knows. He doesn't want you to be just as powerful as He is. Why should He share that kind of knowledge and power with anyone else? So to keep that from happening, He told you not to eat the fruit on this tree.

"But besides being beautiful, you look to be very intelligent. So tell me, does it seem fair that God should keep you from realizing your full potential? Does it seem right that He should keep all this power and knowledge to Himself ? Maybe you don't really know God as well as you think you do.

"Here," the serpent said, picking a piece of fruit and placing it in Eve's hand, "go ahead and try it. You have nothing to lose—and everything to gain!"

The serpent made sense, Eve thought. Why else would God keep them from this tree if not to hoard its benefits for Himself? Apparently God had not been fully open and fair with them.

Eve took a bite, then another. She savored the exotic new flavor and thought she felt a wave of energy surging through her. She was sure the sensation indicated that her migration to a higher plane of consciousness had begun.

Later that same day, as Lucifer and his forces gleefully celebrated their great victory, Adam and Eve heard God calling to them in the Garden of Eden. Normally when He called, they ran gladly to meet Him. But this evening, they "hid themselves from the presence of the Lord God amongst the trees of the garden." Genesis 3:8, KJV.

"Where are you?" God called to them.

"I heard your voice," Adam finally answered, "and I was *afraid.*" See Genesis 3:9.

Adam, afraid of God?

A Cat Named Mittens

Which brings me to Mittens. Mittens and I got along famously until the day I took her to the vet. Our little striped cat with the white feet had reached that point in life when she wanted to become a mother.

I had other ideas.

Having never been in a car before, she meowed piteously all the way to the clinic. Several hours later I picked up a very groggy kitty, now minus a few key parts, and we drove back home.

But when the effects of the anesthesia wore off, I quickly discovered that somehow the relationship I had enjoyed with Mittens had fundamentally changed. No sooner would I approach her than she would race for cover, then warn me with loud hisses, bared fangs, and raised fur to keep my distance.

As Mittens had worked things out in her little feline mind, I was now the Great Villain. Had I not, after all, wrenched her unceremoniously from the security of her familiar surroundings and carried her off, trembling in terror, in a strange moving room? Had I not then taken her from the moving room into another strange place where dogs barked, placed her in the hands of strange people—and simply left her? And at length had I not brought her home again—all foggy-minded and hurting—in the strange moving room?

What I had done with only her best good in mind, Mittens held decidedly against me. And even though I fully understood why she scrambled in fright to get away from me whenever I appeared, I was saddened that she couldn't realize that I was still very much her friend.

I determined to win back her friendship. After many months, a day came when she actually let me touch her for a moment. And in time she relaxed enough not to panic at my footsteps, enough to let me once again stroke her smooth fur.

Mittens still has a way to go before she feels totally at ease with me again. But we're getting there.

A Broken Relationship

Most of us alive on this planet have a way to go yet, too, if we are ever to feel at ease with God again. Ever since that day in Eden, we've been uneasy around Him—even afraid of Him. Somehow sin is like that. Sin brings a break in our relationship with our Maker that causes us to see Him, not as He really is, but in a totally false light.

A signboard in front of a large city church once asked: "Does God seem far away? Who do you think moved?" Sin brings a separation between us and our God. It brings a fundamental change into the relationship He originally intended for us to enjoy with Him. But the separation is not because God moves away from us. Sin is what happens when we move away from Him.

Sin is choosing to live apart from our only source of life and true happiness.

When I took our cat Mittens to the vet, our relationship suffered some heavy-duty damage. And when human beings sinned, the same thing happened to our relationship with God.

I don't know what your picture of God is at the moment. But I do know that if you are in the least afraid of Him, angry at Him, uneasy around Him, it is because the separation of sin is keeping you from seeing Him as He really is.

Separated from God, we begin to imagine all sorts of things about Him that simply are not true. We begin to blame Him for the pain our own sin brings us. We come to see Him as basically *against* us—as our stern judge or frowning Father, if not our outright enemy.

And in creating these false pictures of God, we have a lot of help. Satan, the fallen Lucifer, is constantly at work slinging mud at God's reputation to picture Him as the worst of villains. Satan is consumed with the goal of making God look bad. So when trouble invades our lives—tragedy, pain, illness, grief—he immediately presses us to put the blame on God.

If you were a good father, and your children rebelled and ran away from you, how would you feel? And if they ran from you like frightened animals whenever you approached, what would you do?

When it happened to God, He determined to win the rebels back. Even though *we* broke the relationship, *He* took the initiative to heal it again. He did what must be done when *any* relationship breaks down: He began to *communicate*. He would combat the devil's lies with the truth about Himself. He knew we were afraid, insecure, alienated, distrustful.

So God spoke two mighty, healing words.

Chapter 4
Two Words

Ronald Reagan's answers to my questions were witty and eminently quotable. He continued his friendly banter even as we stood shaking hands for the photographer.

Now, should you wonder if indeed I ever really interviewed President Reagan in the White House Oval Office, let me assure you that I did not. I interviewed Ronald Reagan in Pope Valley, California—and he wasn't to become President of the United States for another fifteen years.

The year was 1965, and Ronald Reagan was running for his first term as governor of California. I learned that he would be making a campaign stop in Pope Valley—a small hamlet a few miles downhill from Pacific Union College. And as editor of the student newspaper there, I determined to wangle an interview with the candidate—and much to my surprise and delight, succeeded.

Even then, Reagan exuded that personal magnetism—that indefinable quality called "charisma"—that would eventually help him win the presidency.

The Charismatic Carpenter

The charisma of a Reagan or a Kennedy or a Churchill is an uncommon quality in the world's public figures. Only a few in each generation seem to possess it. But of all the charismatic personalities this world has known, the magnetism of one dwarfs all the others.

He was not a president. He was not a military leader. He was not an actor or corporate CEO or a billionaire tycoon. He was a young and poor Middle Eastern carpenter without a college degree.

He has been known by many names—one of which is "the Word of God." See John 1:1-3. The Word. Why would anyone be called "the Word"? A word, of course, is the basic unit of speech. Speech conveys thought. Speech *communicates*. And communication is the great healer of broken relationships.

The outrageous lies of Eden had done their damnable work, turning the trust and love of Adam and Eve to suspicion and fear. But God would not let the lies go unanswered. Though His children were alienated and separated from Him now by a cold barrier of sin, He *would* get through to them with the truth. He would speak healing words powerful enough to counteract—and ultimately destroy—the deadly sin virus that had invaded His creation.

To win His created children back—to set the record straight—the Father would rely on the awesome power of two words. And His first great Word was "*the* Word"—Jesus Christ the Son of God.

In Eden, Lucifer implied to Adam and Eve that God could not be trusted—that He did not have their highest happiness in mind. He convinced them that God was selfishly and unfairly holding out on them— and that He had lied to them about death resulting from eating the forbidden fruit.

And ever since Eden, Lucifer has painted God as a villain to those of us who have descended from Adam and Eve. He paints God as arbitrary, as issuing commands and making rules that have no reason but to prove that He is in charge. He paints God as severe, as an autocratic and ruthless judge just waiting to throw the book at us for our smallest mistakes. He paints God as distant, as Someone who cares so little about us that He watches from the sidelines as we hurt and grieve and struggle.

Lucifer's Self-Portrait

But Lucifer the devil, Satan the serpent, is an abysmally poor painter. His portrayal of God's character is, in fact, a self-portrait which He attempts to pass off as a perfect representation of the Father.

God sent Jesus the Word to paint, not with brushes but with His words and His life, a true picture of the Father's character. And every day of our lives, you and I are confronted by the two contrasting pictures of God. By deliberate choice or by default, we vote daily as to which picture is the true likeness of our Father in Heaven. And the importance of that daily vote is too great to calculate. Because how we vote will ultimately determine not only our own eternal destiny, but the outcome of the great cosmic battle between Christ and Satan.

In time, Jesus arrived here on Earth to show us what God was really like. He painted the clearest picture of the Father this world has ever seen.

"God was reconciling the world to himself in Christ." 2 Corinthians 5:19. God never needed to be reconciled to us. He isn't the one who left us—we left Him. God has never changed His opinion about us—we are the ones who have changed our opinion about Him. God doesn't need to be persuaded to take us back—but we need to be persuaded that He *wants* us back.

"Anyone who has seen me," Jesus said, "has seen the Father." John 14:9. And what do we see when we see Jesus? We see love and warmth and acceptance and sympathy and forgiveness. We see a God who became one of us and spent His every waking hour, not in pursuing His own happiness, but in trying to maximize ours. We see Someone who seemed to be saying, "You can reject and neglect and ignore Me. You can claim I don't exist. You can use the breath I have given you to curse Me. You can join forces with My sworn enemy to slander My name. You can spit full in My face and hang Me between Heaven and Earth to die. But there is one thing you can never do. And that is to make Me stop loving you."

The Second Word

Jesus was and is the Word. But God spoke another Word in His efforts to win us back. That Word is, of course, the Bible. Through these two Words, God speaks directly to you and to me, showing us His love, healing the rift in our relationship, calling us home.

God did not send the Bible to us by overnight express from Heaven. He did not hire a staff of temporary secretaries to take word-for-word dictation. Instead, He inspired the minds of the Bible's writers with His thoughts and messages, which they then wrote out in their own words. Thus, while the Bible had many writers, it really had only one Author.

The entire Bible—Old and New Testaments—though expressed in human language, is an infallible revelation of God's will and character. For those who accept it and its Author, the Bible is the final authority on Earth as to what is true (what to believe) and what is right (how to live).

The central personality of the Written Word is the Living Word—Jesus Christ. And the central theme of the Bible is God's love for us as demonstrated in the life, death, and teachings of Jesus.

Being a large book, the Bible covers a lot of territory. It contains history and prophecy and doctrine, biography and poetry and counsel. But for many, the chief motive for reading the Bible is not so much to learn its facts as to become acquainted with its Author. Through prayerfully studying the Bible, any one of us can communicate once again with our Father, carrying on a conversation as real as with anyone else we know.

As the Bible helps us to see God as He really is, our opinion of Him begins to change. We begin to lose our fear of Him. We find ourselves wanting the broken relationship to be restored. And if we continue spending time getting to know God through the Word, the powerful revelation of His love it contains will profoundly change us. This radical change the Bible calls being "born again."

The Bible is just like any other book published on Earth in that it contains printed words on paper between two covers. But it is unlike any other book on Earth in that it cannot be correctly understood or truly appreciated without the direct guidance of its Author.

Those who come to the Bible simply to find ammunition for their religious arguments will surely miss God's message. Those who search its pages only to find support for what they already believe will also miss God's message. Those who elect themselves judges as to what parts of the Bible to accept and what parts to reject will ensure that they miss God's message. But those who come to the Bible with a driving need to get acquainted with their Father will hear His message. And that message will win them back.

The Bible contains many teachings—or doctrines—on a wide variety of subjects. It is possible for a person to become an expert on the doctrines of the Bible without ever being changed by them. But the truth is that the doctrines of the Bible are not simply systematized religious information. Each doctrine of the Bible presents one more picture of a loving, caring God.

Wrongly viewed or studied, even a Bible doctrine can present a false picture of what God is like. But studied with prayer and humility—and with the Author's immediate guidance—each Bible doctrine and each Bible story becomes a picture that helps us see God more clearly.

In the aftermath of Eden's disaster, God spoke two mighty, healing words. But His words would not go unanswered.

Database 5, File T-8835.300, Record 416
[Third Century, A.D.]
Strategy Directive 7552.401
RE: Propaganda

He calls his book of lies "the word" and "the truth." I call it propaganda. It's a whitewash, a cover-up, a snow job. If it's truth the Targets want, we'll give them our truth. If it's words they want to hear, we'll keep the words coming until they forget anything the enemy ever said.

We're at war here—never forget that. And we have no weapons more powerful than words. The book of lies says that in the beginning was the word. The enemy may think he had the first word. But I vow to you once again that I will have the last one.

Lucifer,
Commander-in-chief, Imperial Forces
King of Earth
Most High God in Exile
UNIVERSAL EMPIRE

Chapter 5
Newton's Third Law

OK, class—listen up. Today we study McFarland's First Law of Motion, which is: *Never get on an amusement ride unless someone is holding a gun on you.*

Case in point number one: Several years ago our family spent a Sunday at the state fair, and in time we drifted over to the midway rides.

"Daddy, I want to ride on that," my little girl announced. She pointed to a contraption called the Roundup—a big circular floor with walls all around the perimeter. Afraid that Dana might not be quite up to the ride on her own, I volunteered to go with her in case she became frightened or queasy.

Forty or fifty of us trooped in and—facing the center—stood against the walls and took hold of the handles on either side of us. Soon the whole business began to spin, gradually picking up speed. As the ride accelerated, my stomach and semicircular canals went to red alert. But the worst was yet to come.

When the monster was rotating fast enough that we were all plastered firmly against the walls, the floor dropped out from under us. Somewhere I heard a lot of screaming, but by now I was too nauseated to join in. Nonetheless, I forced myself to turn my head to ask Dana how she was doing.

"Oh, great! This is fun!" she chirped. I was glad to be of help.

Just then the whirling mechanical dervish began to tilt. They were going to turn it up on edge! Before long I found myself looping through approximately the same pattern of motion as would be described by a fly superglued to the end of a moving propeller.

After what seemed like several decades of abject misery, somebody somewhere finally lowered the ride, brought up the floor, and mercifully slowed the infernal thing to a stop. I staggered off with an advanced case of vertigo. The ground in front of me swirled and reeled, and it would be hours before my stomach came in for a landing.

"Daddy, Daddy! Can we go again? Can we?"

Yes, indeed. Dana certainly had been lucky that I went along. How could she have made it without me?

Case in point number two: On a recent business trip to southern California, an artist friend and I found ourselves in Anaheim with a free day on our hands. In order to get a cheaper air fare, we'd had to stay over a weekend.

So we did the obviously logical thing and sallied forth to "do Disneyland." About an hour or two into our great adventure, we arrived at a circular building called Space Mountain, from which the rather constant, muffled sound of screaming emanated.

"Listen to those silly girls," I remarked to Tim as we waited in line. "If it was half as bad as they make it sound, no one would ever ride these things."

At the head of the line, we found a little train of two-seat cars like those you see on roller coasters— and the two of us climbed into one and pulled the bar down in front of us. With a lurch, the cars leaped forward, and we headed down the straight track through a low door. Once past the door, everything went pitch black, and within seconds I realized I had made one of the greatest mistakes of my life.

I still don't know exactly what went on in there, but it felt like riding a roller coaster at 500 miles an hour through hairpin turns and sudden steep drop-offs—all in total darkness. I would gladly have bellowed along with the silly screaming girls, but my vocal cords were paralyzed.

My life flashed before me. I repented of everything I'd ever done and a few things I'd only thought of doing. I wondered how my family would get along without me. I wished a noisome pox on the house of Disney.

And finally, as the berserk train of Space Mountain accelerated to the speed of light—all the while executing right-angle turns and 500-foot drop-offs—I numbly gave myself last rites and prepared to meet my Maker. Anytime now I expected to be thrown from the flimsy little car to sail off into the jet-black void. Someday they would find my body on the floor of hollow Space Mountain. My face would be frozen into a mask of nausea and terror.

Now, if any of you out there in reader-land have ever been through Space Mountain and lived to claim you enjoyed it, be my guest. As for me, I'd far rather spend all eternity munching shards of broken glass than to ever get near that diabolical ride again.

To review, then. McFarland's First Law of Motion: Never get on an amusement ride unless someone is holding a gun on you. And even then, I'd take some time to weigh the options.

Another physical law is perhaps better known to

most of you. Known as Newton's Third Law of Motion, it states that for every action, there is an equal and opposite reaction. And to return now to the arena of serious discussion, I'd like to observe that what Isaac Newton discovered to be true in the physical realm seems to have its parallel in the spiritual realm. Because for every action God takes, Satan weighs in with an opposing reaction.

In creating Earth—with all its natural beauty, its perfect plant, animal, and human life—God acted, and how! And Satan lost no time in moving to react. What God had created, he would destroy. What God had called good, he would ruin.

The Legacy of Eden

At least four great truths of the Bible can be traced all the way back to Eden. And the fallen Lucifer has attacked these truths all through the centuries since. So successful have his efforts been that the overwhelming majority of Earth's population have accepted the devil's lies in place of these truths of Eden.

The first great truth Satan has attacked is the truth of creation.

Database 3, File R-4380.721, Record 38
[Shortly after the fall of Adam and Eve]
Strategy Directive 3888.74
RE: The Grand Strategy

From the beginning, I have stressed to you that our Grand Strategy is to make the enemy look his worst in the estimation of all intelligent beings in the universe. He must be seen as unfair, as someone who cares only for himself, and as a liar.

I want each of you constantly to be thinking of the best ways to minimize or neutralize the impact of anything the enemy says or does. When it comes to either an action or stated position of the enemy, ask yourselves such questions as the following:

Can we attack it directly?
Can we attract attention away from it?
Can we counterfeit it?
Can we compromise it?
Can we deny that it exists?
Can we ridicule it?
Can we slowly change it into something else?
Can we claim it never happened?
Can we make it seem irrelevant?

Take, for example, the idea that the enemy created Earth and all life on it. Our work is to begin immediately to see that the Targets lose sight of this. How can this be done? I want you to think this through and be prepared to propose your ideas at the next CIS meeting.

Lucifer,
Commander-in-chief, Imperial Forces
King of Earth
Most High God in Exile
UNIVERSAL EMPIRE

Database 5, File B-22905.327, Record 4
[Late 1980s]
Strategy Directive 2975.84
RE: Update on the Creation Myth

Our strategy to destroy the idea of a literal creation by

the enemy is well on track. The influence of our agent Darwin continues to be felt. The concept of evolution is firmly entrenched.

I am especially pleased with the results of our counter-creation campaign in the more developed areas of Earth. In these places, creation is now seen as a delusion of the uneducated—as the comforting self-deception of the scientifically uninformed. And in these areas, the evolutionary idea—that Targets developed over millions of years from electrified one-celled sea life, on up through salamanders and finally apes—is accepted largely without question.

Our agent theologians continue to be of great service to us as they convince the Targets under their influence that the first few chapters of Genesis in the book of lies are mythical. It is vital that Targets not believe this account to be literal history.

Remember, if Targets can be convinced that creation never happened, they can usually also be convinced that the enemy doesn't exist. And if we can convince them of this, we have then effectively shut them off from communication with him—and then we have them.

For those Targets who stubbornly cling to the creation idea, our efforts must be to convince them that our enemy is truly their enemy as well.

Lucifer,
Commander-in-chief, Imperial Forces
King of Earth
Most High God in Exile
UNIVERSAL EMPIRE

A few years back, I subscribed to no less than three science magazines. Two of them have since folded, but I still take the survivor—*Discover* magazine.

I enjoy reading about everything from robotics to superconductivity, from AIDS research to space exploration, from high tech to the fate of the dinosaurs.

One unsettling fact that emerges from reading these magazines, however, is that today's scientific community is virtually unanimous in dismissing the Genesis story of creation as unworthy of serious consideration. The evolutionary model of origins is not only endorsed, it is *assumed*.

The October 1985 issue of *Science Digest*, for example, featured as its cover article "The 20 Greatest Unanswered Questions of Science." Some of these questions, with their opening paragraphs:

How Did Life Begin?—"Sometime between Earth's beginning 4.6 billion years ago and the date that the oldest primitive algae and bacteria became fossilized a billion years later, our earliest ancestor was born: the first self-replicating cell."

Where Did Intelligent Life Come From?—"Some 5 million years ago, our ancestors stepped out of the forest onto the savanna—and shifted the course of history. Life in the open had profound effects upon these primates."

How Did Apes Lead to Man?—"Where man came from has been the subject of speculation since the dawn of history. While scientists still don't know the answer—and fundamentalists cling to a belief in divine creation—a detailed picture of man's early days is emerging."

The cover billboarding on the September 1986 *Discover* states the following modern confession: "We no longer know who gave rise to whom—perhaps not even how, or when, we came into being."

Were it not for the success of Satan's attacks on the story of divine creation told in Genesis, such confusion and uncertainty as to the origin of man, Earth, and the universe would not exist.

The Bible is certain, unconfused, unequivocal:

In the beginning God created the heavens and the earth. Genesis 1:1.

The Lord God formed man from the dust of the ground and breathed into his nostrils the breath of life, and man became a living being. Genesis 2:7.

He spoke, and it came to be; he commanded, and it stood firm. Psalm 33:9.

In the beginning was the Word, . . . and the Word was God. . . . Through him all things were made; without him nothing was made that has been made. John 1:1-3.

Sex, Marriage, and the Family

The second great truth that can be traced back to Eden is the truth about sex, marriage, and the family. As Dr. Charles Wittschiebe noted in his book of the same title, God invented sex. This apparently comes as a major revelation to Madison Avenue, Hollywood, and each new generation of teenagers.

As God made it, sex was not dirty or "unspiritual." It was not something to feel guilty about. It could not be associated with sleaze, lust, or perversion. Not, that is, until the devil moved in on it.

Database 3, File C-9147.303, Record 119
[Shortly after the fall]
Strategy Directive 2007.21
RE: Sex and Marriage

Even though we are not humans and are therefore somewhat at a disadvantage in fully understanding this whole phenomenon of sex, reproduction, and marriage, it obviously holds fantastic potential to be useful to us in turning the Targets against the enemy.

As for sex, we must convince the Targets that the enemy strongly disapproves of it. We must encourage them to separate it from both love and marriage. Encourage them to see sex in terms of self-gratification rather than as an expression of so-called love. Particularly for those Targets under the greatest influence of the enemy, present sex as intrinsically evil and inimical to "spirituality"—and thus make sex without guilt difficult if not impossible.

Since the enemy apparently intends sex to involve the total person and to take place in the context of a marriage relationship, we must do our utmost to reduce sex primarily to a physical pleasure and to separate it from relationships—especially the marriage relationship.

And as for marriage, since the enemy apparently sees this relationship in terms of a permanent commitment and as a sort of "laboratory of love," we must attack marriage with every resource at our disposal. Make it seem unnecessary, irrelevant, and confining. Turn every possible marriage into an ongoing war by encouraging the selfishness of the two Targets involved. Play up the advantages of a relationship without commitment or responsibility.

My next directive will contain my thoughts on how we can attack the family structure.

Lucifer,
Commander-in-chief, Imperial Forces
King of Earth
Most High God in Exile
UNIVERSAL EMPIRE

As to how well the rebel angel and his forces have succeeded in implementing their war against sex, marriage, and the family—you be the judge.

Two other truths of Eden are also under special attack by Satan and his militant followers today. And amazingly, when Satan moves against these two truths, his motion is seconded from Christian pulpits the world around. As you would correctly and brilliantly deduce, these beleaguered truths will be the focus of the chapters immediately ahead.

Chapter 6
The Late Average Joe

Meet Joe.

Joe seems normal, ordinary, and—well, sort of like your average Joe. But the fact is that Joe has one quirk that makes you wonder sometimes if his elevator goes all the way to the top.

You see, Joe goes through life exactly one day late—even in leap years. Which means that he celebrates New Year's Day on January 2, Independence Day on July 5, Christmas on December 26, and—you get the idea.

Being one day out of sync has its disadvantages. Joe always puts out the trash the day after it's been picked up. When he goes to a football game, he has the whole stadium to himself. And he hurries each year to get his income tax to the IRS by April 16.

Each Tuesday morning, he shows up faithfully for a new week of work. And when the Lord's Day rolls around and he goes to church, there's nobody there, right?

Wrong.

Every week the church is packed. But why? If Joe is always 24 hours late, why wouldn't the church be empty? The fact that the church is full, as *Star Trek's* Mr. Spock would say, is not logical.

Well, to this apparent inconsistency, there is an answer. Be patient, because it may take another page or two to get at it. But let's get started. And the place to start is where we left off in the last chapter—the book of Genesis. Consider now another of the Eden truths Satan hates.

> The heavens and the earth were completed in all their vast array. By the seventh day God had finished the work he had been doing; so on the seventh day he rested from all his work. And God blessed the seventh day and made it holy, because on it he rested from all the work of creating that he had done. Genesis 2:1-3.

May I direct your attention to the word *rested* that shows up twice in the verses above? Did God rest because He was tired? Apparently not, for in another place the Bible says:

> Do you not know? Have you not heard? The Lord is the everlasting God, the Creator of the ends of the earth. *He will not grow tired or weary*, and his understanding no one can fathom. Isaiah 40:28, emphasis supplied.

Finished Work

What does it mean, then, when it says God "rested"? It means that He was no longer working, because His work was done. When I turn off my car engine, I can accurately say that the engine is at rest. It is no longer moving—no longer working.

Now notice something else with me about that word *rested*. The original book of Genesis was written, not in English, but in Hebrew. And in Hebrew, the word translated in English as "rest" is *shabath*. And *shabath* also comes over into English as "sabbath." So "sabbath" and "rest" mean the same thing.

With that little word study out of the way, let's return to our original text in Genesis. "On the seventh day," Genesis 2:2 says, God "rested from all his work." God rested. He "sabbathed," if you will.

Thousands of years later, God delivered His chosen people Israel from over 400 years in captivity to the Egyptians. As He led them through the Sinai Desert to the Promised Land, He found it necessary to restate His Ten Commandments to them. During their long stay in Egypt, the Israelites had just about forgotten everything they had ever known about God.

So God reminded them of His law as they were camped at the base of Mount Sinai. And the fourth of the Ten Commandments said:

> Remember the Sabbath day by keeping it holy.
> Six days you shall labor and do all your work,
> but the seventh day is a Sabbath to the Lord
> your God. On it you shall not do any work,
> neither you, nor your son or daughter, nor your
> manservant or maidservant, nor your animals,
> nor the alien within your gates. For in six days
> the Lord made the heavens and the earth, the
> sea, and all that is in them, but he rested on
> the seventh day. Therefore the Lord blessed
> the Sabbath day and made it holy. Exodus
> 20:8-11.

Now, I should let you know at this point that some people today say that God gave the seventh-day Sabbath just to the Israelites at Sinai—that it was an exclusively Jewish day. But we've already seen from the Bible that the Sabbath began over 2000 years earlier at creation—so that idea doesn't really hold up. Notice, too, that when God reminded Israel about the Sabbath, He said, *"Remember* the Sabbath day." And it's hard to remember something you've never heard of before.

According to both Genesis and Exodus, *when* is the Sabbath? The seventh day. Now, find a calendar. What is the seventh day of every week? Saturday, right? So is Saturday the seventh-day Sabbath? But don't most people go to church on *Sunday*? What's going on here?

Two possibilities are open to us:

1. Someone has changed our calendar so that Saturday, not Sunday, is the seventh day of the week.

2. Someone has changed the Sabbath, or Lord's Day, from Saturday the seventh day to Sunday the first day of the week.

When the Calendar Was Changed

Has our calendar been changed? The answer is Yes—once. Back in A.D. 1582, Pope Gregory XIII decreed that the day following Thursday, October 4, 1582 would be Friday, October 15, 1582. The reasons for this are a bit too complicated to detail here, but suffice it to say that because too many leap years had been observed over the centuries prior to 1582, the calendar was out of step with the true astronomical clock. Gregory's change corrected the count, and we've been basically on track ever since.

But note that the weekly cycle was not interrupted. Thursday was still followed by Friday, Friday by

Saturday, Saturday by Sunday. In fact, a little research will prove that the weekly cycle has never been changed in all of human history. The seventh day, in other words, has always been Saturday.

Then what about the second possibility? Has someone attempted to change the Sabbath from Saturday to Sunday? And, surprisingly, the answer is Yes. But that someone was not God. The Bible knows nothing of a change in the Sabbath. While here on Earth, Jesus said:

> Do not think that I have come to abolish the Law or the Prophets; I have not come to abolish them but to fulfill them. Matthew 5:17.

When Jesus was crucified, the Bible says that He died on Friday, the preparation day, that He rested in the tomb on Saturday, the Sabbath of the commandment, and that He was resurrected on Sunday, the first day of the week. See Luke 23:52 to 24:1.

To learn of the change of the Sabbath, we must go to history. And here we discover that in the centuries immediately following the death of Christ's apostles, observance of the Sabbath gradually transferred from Saturday to Sunday. This came about as a result of both church and government decrees. (The full story of this change is fascinating, but far too detailed to include here. For a fine overview of this incredible metamorphosis, I recommend George E. Vandeman's book *When God Made Rest.**)

So, you see, even though most Christians today attend church on Sunday and sincerely believe they are observing the Lord's Day, that simply is not the case.

---

* *When God Made Rest*, by George E. Vandeman. Copyright 1987 by Pacific Press Publishing Association, Boise, Idaho.

Many assume that somewhere, the New Testament supports a change of the Sabbath from Saturday the seventh day to Sunday the first day—as a memorial of Christ's resurrection. And that, my friends, is why Joe can be moving through life one day late and find the church full when he shows up Sunday morning!

Memorial of Creation

But the Bible says the Sabbath is a memorial of *creation*, not of Christ's resurrection. Notice again the reason the fourth commandment gives for keeping the Sabbath:

> In six days the Lord made the heavens and the earth, the sea, and all that is in them, but he rested on the seventh day. Therefore the Lord blessed the Sabbath day and made it holy. Exodus 20:11.

The Sabbath is a weekly reminder to us that God is our Creator. And can it really be just coincidental that as human beings have lost sight of God's true Sabbath, they have also lost sight of the truth of creation—of which the Sabbath was to be a weekly reminder?

God did not give us the Sabbath as a duty—but as a gift. And this gift does more than remind us constantly that God is our Father and Creator. As well as being a memorial of creation, the Sabbath was to be a symbol of sanctification. See Ezekiel 20:12, 20 and Exodus 31:13.

Now, sanctification is one of those big theological words, but its meaning isn't complicated. It has to do with how God sets us apart to cleanse our lives from sinning and to use us in His service. And if you've ever tried to quit sinning on your own, you know what a doomed effort that is. Sanctification is abandoning our efforts to clean ourselves up so we can come to Jesus, in favor of coming to Jesus so He can clean us up. And the Sabbath is a weekly reminder to us that He is our Sanctifier.

Finally, the Sabbath, as we've already noticed, is all about rest. See Hebrews, chapter 4. And we're not talking here simply about physical rest. The Sabbath is primarily about *spiritual* rest—about quitting the hard work we put forth on our own to keep God's laws, to grow more like Christ, to overcome our sins.

The Sabbath reminds us that we can rest from our own efforts to make ourselves acceptable to God. For one thing, we are *already* accepted, even though we are still sinners. See Ephesians 1:6 and Romans 5:8. And for another, only through God's power can any spiritual improvement happen in our lives.

Database 5, File Y-1136.009, Record 3
[Late 1980s]
Imperial Order 413.6
RE: The Sabbath

Over the past 2,000 years, our efforts against the sabbath have been particularly successful. Today the majority of Earth's population is non-Christian, and only a tiny minority of Christian Targets stubbornly persist in keeping the enemy's sabbath.

We must continue to remind any doubters that it is inconceivable that such an overwhelming majority of the Christian world could be wrong about their day of worship. Continue suggesting the idea that all that really matters is keeping one day out of seven.

Present Saturday sabbath keeping as legalism, as an outdated relic of Judaism, as ultimately divisive to the church at large. Bring intense social and economic pressure to bear on those who refuse to give it up.

i sense that our long war with the enemy is nearly over. What we do, we must do quickly. With this order, I am establishing a subcommittee of our main sabbath task force to develop a final detailed battle plan to overthrow the sabbath (subcommittee membership attached).

If taken seriously, we all know how damaging the sabbath can be to us. We know that it is altogether too effective in keeping Targets from seeing the enemy as we want them to see him. We must double and triple our efforts to make observance of our counterfeit universal.

As you know, we have succeeded in influencing many prominent Target theologians and clergymen to press for legislated morality (school prayers and abortion, for example). Perhaps the time has come for us aggressively to reintroduce the idea of legislating observance of our sabbath. I will personally place this at the top of the agenda for the new subcommittee.

Lucifer,
Commander-in-chief, Imperial Forces
King of Earth
Most High God in Exile
UNIVERSAL EMPIRE

Creation.
Sex, Marriage, and the Family.
The Sabbath.

The legacy of Eden under attack. But the self-styled king of Earth continues also today to trumpet his most brazen lie—which happens to be the first lie any human being ever heard.

Chapter 7
Echoes of Eden

From my window-seat vantage point aboard US Air Flight 317 from Syracuse, I could take in the entire sweep of the island of Manhattan. As our DC-9 banked into its final approach to LaGuardia Airport, I looked down on the Statue of Liberty, the World Trade Center towers, and further up the island, the familiar spire of the Empire State Building.

Soon the crowded houses and apartments of Brooklyn and Queens raced by beneath us. Then, only moments before touchdown, I saw it. A very large cemetery. Thousands, probably tens of thousands of headstones seemed to stretch nearly to the horizon. And as our plane settled onto the runway, my thoughts remained focused on what I had just seen.

Each grave marker represented a human life that undoubtedly had once been celebrated with great joy at birth. Each cold stone represented what had once been a warm, feeling, living, breathing human being.

But now they lived and breathed no more. Disease, accidents, violence, war, disasters, and old age had claimed them. And each granite monument also meant grief and tears and heartbreak for loved ones left behind.

In the field of stone pillars in Queens, I read once

again my own sure fate. For unless my lifetime is interrupted by the return of Christ to Earth, the path of my days ahead leads inexorably to the grave.

But that certainly isn't how God originally planned it. God created human beings to live forever—ageless, tireless, surging with energy. Only one thing could change all that. Sin. So God plainly warned our first parents—"If you sin, you will die. See Genesis 2:17.

God did not say, "If you sin, I will kill you," or, "If you sin, I will punish you with death." He was simply saying that sin kills. The inescapable consequence of sin is death.

The First Great Lie

But Satan wants us to believe that sin is basically harmless—that we may enjoy its pleasures with no fear of its penalty. So with God's warning to Adam and Eve still fresh in their memories, Satan countered with the first great lie in human history.

God: "You will surely die." Genesis 2:17.
Satan: "You will not surely die." Genesis 3:4.

Direct contradiction! Branding God a liar! But it worked. And incredibly, today it is Satan's version of truth that prevails almost universally—even in the Christian church. Man, we are told even from Christian pulpits, will never die. At death he may shed his body, but his immortal soul lives on forever.

When death claims someone we love, the thought that the separation might be permanent is unbearable. We echo the anguished question of Job: "If a man dies, will he live again?" Job 14:14.

Satan's answer, that no one really dies—that except for our bodies, we will all survive death—*seems* comforting enough. It seems to take much of the sting out of death. And at the countless funerals held every day around the globe, spiritual leaders assure mourners that their loved ones have simply cast aside their bodies but are still very much alive, having ascended into the presence of God Himself.

Near-Death Experiences

People today the world around are enormously curious as to what happens to us when we die. Thus, a book like *Life After Life*, by Dr. Raymond A. Moody, has sold over three-and-a-half million copies and approaches its fortieth printing.

Listen to how Dr. Moody describes death—as gleaned from reports of those who have returned from "clinical death" experiences—on the back cover of his book:

> A man is dying and, as he reaches the point of greatest physical distress, he hears himself pronounced dead by his doctor. He begins to hear an uncomfortable noise, a loud ringing or buzzing, and at the same time feels himself moving very rapidly through a long, dark tunnel. After this, he finds himself outside of his own physical body. . . . Soon, other things begin to happen. Others come to meet and help him. He glimpses the spirits of relatives and friends who have already died, and a loving, warm spirit of a kind he has never encountered before—*a being of light*—appears before him.— *Life After Life*, by Raymond A. Moody, M.D., back cover.

A long, dark tunnel. A being of light. And the reports are all strangely similar. But George Vandeman asks the obvious questions:

> Were these people really dead? Or just *near* death? Evidently they were not irreversibly dead, for all were resuscitated. Evidently these experiences are just the malfunctioning of a mind almost gone. There are many similar out-of-body experiences in drug literature.
>
> But if these stories represent simply the misfiring of a mind near death how is it that hundreds of minds are misfiring in almost the same way? Something is going on here. Something strange. Is it possible that some external power, some intelligent and highly motivated entity, may be stepping in to control these weakened and malfunctioning minds? If so, who would be suspect? Who could be so motivated?—*The Telltale Connection*, by George E. Vandeman, pp. 22, 23.

Who is behind it all? And who, we want to know, is the mysterious "being of light" who appears at the end of the long, dark tunnel? Listen: "And no wonder, for Satan himself masquerades as an angel of light." 2 Corinthians 11:14.

Counterfeit Truth

Do these near-death experiences really *prove* that there is life after death—especially if those involved never really died? And do these experiences, as some say, prove the Bible to be true, when, in fact, they directly contradict the Bible?

You see, for every Bible truth, the devil has a counterfeit. And Satan's counterfeit version of what happens at death is the polar opposite of what the Bible teaches. "The living," says the Bible, "know that they will die, but the dead know nothing." Ecclesiastes 9:5. "Put not your trust in princes," adds the book of Psalms, "nor in the son of man, in whom there is no help. His breath goeth forth, he returneth to his earth; in that very day his thoughts perish." Psalm 146:3, 4, KJV.

Early in human history, Satan succeeded in selling human beings on the idea that we are really immortal souls living in mortal bodies. This idea really took hold when the Greek philosopher Plato advanced the idea of "dualism"—that is, human nature is dual: mortal body plus immortal soul.

But the Bible does not separate man into soul and body. It sees man as a whole, indivisible unit. Instead of teaching that we *have* souls, the Bible teaches that we *are* souls.

"The Lord God formed man of the dust of the ground, and breathed into his nostrils the breath of life; and man became a living soul. Genesis 2:7, KJV. Dust of the ground + Breath of life = A living soul. When God breathed into the lifeless form of Adam the breath of life, Adam became a living soul—or, as the New International Version puts it, "a living being."

Does the Bible teach that our souls are immortal? "The soul that sinneth," Ezekiel replies, "it shall die." Ezekiel 18:20, KJV. And Paul assures us that "all have sinned." Romans 3:23.

The Bible is inescapably clear that we are all mortal—and that only God has immortality. "Shall mortal man be more just than God?" asks Job. Job 4:17, KJV. "God," wrote Paul, is "the blessed and only Ruler, the King of kings and Lord of lords, *who alone is immortal* and who lives in unapproachable light." 1 Timothy 6:15, 16, emphasis supplied.

Do you hear the echoes of Eden? Do you hear the devil not only assuring Eve, "You will not surely die," but in the same breath promising her, "You will be like God"? See Genesis 3:4, 5. Go ahead and sin, he challenges. Not only will you not die—you will be *immortal, like God*! And today the echoes of Satan's voice are heard everywhere. The psychics, the New Age and Eastern religion gurus, the scientists researching death, the preachers in their pulpits—nearly all of them agree: We all live on after death. We are all immortal!

Do Not Pass GO, Do Not Collect $200

Is it not at least passing curious that of those who died in Bible times, not one records having passed through a long, dark tunnel to meet a "being of light" at the other end? Is it not strange that even the holiest of men apparently did not go directly to Heaven when they died? Yet today, no matter how profligate a life a man may have lived, he is preached directly into Paradise at his funeral.

When Jesus resurrected Lazarus after he had been in the tomb for four days, Lazarus brought back no reports of the terrors of hell or the joys of Heaven.

In his Pentecost sermon, Peter referred to King David: "Brothers, I can tell you confidently that the patriarch David died and was buried, and his tomb is here to this day." "For David did not ascend to heaven." Acts 2:29, 34.

And even Jesus Himself, immediately after His resurrection, said to Mary of Magdala, "Do not hold on to me, for I have not yet returned to the Father." John 20:17.

Lazarus, David, and Jesus all died. And the Bible clearly states that none of them went directly to Heaven. Yet today no sooner does a rock star or crime boss die, than a preacher somewhere rushes into supermarket tabloid print to assure us that his immortal soul has winged its way directly into the presence of God. And the echoes of Eden are heard once more.

Jesus called death "sleep." See John 11:11-14. Death is a time of unconscious, oblivious rest in the grave, awaiting the resurrection day when Christ returns to Earth. During that waiting time, those who die remain in their graves. See Job 7:9, 10; 14:12 and 21:32. Then, when Jesus calls His followers to life again, they—along with Christ's followers who are alive to meet Him—will receive immortality. See 1 Corinthians 15:51-55.

I don't know about you, but I am happy that I serve a God who would not compel me after I die to witness the grief of the loved ones who survive me. I am glad that after I die, I will not have to witness from Heaven the continuing sadness, pain, and trouble of those who remain on this sin-wracked Earth. Would that truly be Heaven, after all—or hell?

Recalled From Paradise

Those who choose to believe that at death they go immediately either to Heaven or to hell, face a lot of hard questions. Let's take Lazarus again. Assuming that his soul flew swiftly to Heaven at his death, doesn't it seem monumentally unfair of Christ to recall him from bliss after four days, to live out the rest of his life on this wretched world?

And what about the judgment? If I am assigned immediately to Heaven or hell when I die, why have a future day of judgment to decide belatedly where I should go? If I die and am sent to hell, and then years or decades later in the judgment day it turns out that I really was supposed to be in Heaven all along, what will God say? "I'm sorry"?

On the other hand, imagine how I might feel being reassigned to hell on the judgment day, after all those years in Paradise!

Another problem: Why have a resurrection? If my "soul" has managed to get along in Heaven for hundreds or thousands of years without a body, why do I suddenly need one again on resurrection day?

If I am humbly willing to accept the plain teaching of my Bible about what will happen to me when I die, these difficult questions disappear.

When Jesus stepped forth from His tomb in dazzling glory that long-ago resurrection morning, He did so as the new head of the human race—as the new Adam. The first Adam was taken prisoner by death. The second Adam—in whom God in His reckoning includes us all—defeated death decisively.

Therefore if the head of the race has broken the power of death, it has no power any longer to forever imprison the individual members of that race. Death is reduced to locking up its prisoners only until Jesus comes with the key to set them free. Death is a defeated enemy—and how can we fear a beaten foe!

That Field in Queens

Imagine with me for a moment the day Jesus returns to this Earth. Escorted by countless angels and wearing His crown as King of the universe, He descends till the entire sky is flooded with light. The clear tone of a trumpet reverberates around you, and Jesus shouts, "Awaken, you that sleep in the dust! Arise!"

Suddenly you hear a low rumble and feel the earth move beneath your feet. Headstones topple in that Queens cemetery, in the cemetery just up the hill from my home, in cemeteries and mausoleums and un-marked graves the world over. The sod rolls back. The followers of Jesus live again!

Death, where is your sting? Grave, where is your victory? Against my will you may steal away those I love and lock them up in your prison. But you cannot keep them there. My Jesus will soon be here to set them free!

Chapter 8
The War Behind All Wars

Called out of their late-evening bingo game at the American Legion hall, George and Joy Swift were met by a man with tears streaming down his face.

"What's happened?" George asked anxiously.

"Something terrible," the man replied. "Please— just go home!"

George and Joy ran for their car and sped home, their thoughts and hearts racing. What could have happened? Had the water heater blown up? Had the house caught fire? Had one of the children been hurt?

Earlier in the evening, the Swifts had left four of their five children at home. Fourteen-year-old Steve and twelve-year-old Greg were to babysit their two small sisters, four-year-old Tonya, and Stacy, one-and-a-half.

Less than a month had passed since their oldest child, seventeen-year-old Stephanie, had undergone surgery to remove a cancerous ovarian tumor. The cancer had also been discovered elsewhere in her body, and that night she was confined to her hospital bed as her doctors worked to treat her malignancy with chemotherapy.

The Swifts arrived to find the street in front of their home lined with police cars and ambulances, their lights flashing. They would soon learn to their absolute horror that someone had broken into their home and shot all four of the children to death.

Only twenty days after the funeral, Stephanie—their last child—succumbed to her illness. Returning home from the hospital, the Swifts found a letter in the day's mail from Joy's doctor. Her recent pap smear had tested positive for cancer of the cervix—she would need to come in immediately.

Joy would ultimately win her own battle with cancer and would in time give birth to three more children. But the aching void in her heart never completely leaves. She and George will never fully forget.*

The 130-year-old red-brick town house on West 10th Street in Greenwich Village had once been home to Mark Twain. But now in response to a 911 call, police and an ambulance raced toward it through the streets of New York City.

This would not be the first time police had been summoned to this address. Frequently, in response to the phone calls of worried neighbors, police had been dispatched to check on reports of screaming and crashing noises coming from apartment 3W. Joel Steinberg, a criminal attorney, shared the apartment with his common-law wife Hedda Nussbaum and their two adoptive children—six-year-old Lisa and sixteen-month-old Mitchell.

Repeatedly, police had found clear evidence that Steinberg was a merciless wife beater, but could do little, as Nussbaum steadfastly refused to press charges.

---

* The full story of the Swift family tragedy is contained in the book "They're All Dead, Aren't They" by Joy Swift. Copyright 1986 by Pacific Press Publishing Association, Boise, Idaho.

This time when they arrived, police found the tall, burly Steinberg standing in the apartment, the limp body of his daughter Lisa in his arms. She had stopped breathing, but the officers could detect a weak pulse. As they worked desperately to revive her, they also noticed that her battered body was covered with welts and bruises.

Lisa was rushed to St. Vincent's Hospital, but the doctors knew immediately that they could do nothing for her. A brain hemorrhage brought on by repeated blows to the head had left her clinically dead. Her death became official when she was disconnected three days later from artificial life support. Baby Mitchell was removed from the home, and Steinberg and Nussbaum were charged with murder.

I don't know about you, but when I hear stories like these, my heart is moved by a whole range of intense emotions, and my mind is filled with questions—not all of which I can answer.

When I first read Joy Swift's story in manuscript, my heart ached and grieved along with hers at their unbelievable loss. And my mind asked Why? The senseless slaying of their children seemed so unthinkably savage—the incredible series of tragedies this one couple endured so utterly unfair.

And when I first read the tragic story of little Lisa Steinberg in the November 23, 1987 issue of *People* magazine—and studied the photo of her innocent face taken three days before her death—I was overcome by very similar feelings and questions. I felt loathing for Joel Steinberg and rage toward him for his repulsive deed. Upon reflection, of course, I realized that there might be much in his life and background that I did not know which, while it might not excuse it, might help explain his monstrous behavior.

I felt a pity and grief for little Lisa too deep for words—almost as if she had been my own child. And my mind again asked its questions. How could such a sweet, innocent child be the object of such an unspeakably brutal crime? What inconceivable hell must this little girl have lived in? And again, Why? Yes, especially, WHY? *Why did God let this happen?*

An Anguished Question

These two true stories, unfortunately, represent only a single drop in the sea of trouble and sorrow and suffering that sweeps unceasingly over the face of our planet. The collective daily burden of both reported and unreported misery borne by Earth's inhabitants is too staggering to calculate or comprehend. And from all points of the globe we may hear the anguished question arising—"Why?" Why do so many innocent people suffer? If there is a God—and if He cares at all—why does He let these things happen?

I'd like to suggest that only as we see the events of our lives against the backdrop of the great conflict between Christ and Satan can we ever begin to understand the "why" of suffering and tragedy. Only as these things are seen in their larger context do they begin to make any sense. Without the perspective provided by the "larger view" of this great cosmic battle, most of what happens to us here seems maddeningly random, senseless, capricious.

But do bad things happen to us for no reason? Has the world gone berserk and God stands by sympathetically but helplessly wringing His hands, unable to do anything about it? Worse, could God intervene but doesn't care enough to get involved? Or worse still, is there no God there and, as some tell us, we must learn to bear our existential pain alone?

One book of the Bible opens perhaps the clearest window on this whole question of the "why" of suffering. Sometime after the debacle of Eden, God called the angels together, and guess who invited himself to the meeting?

"One day the angels came to present themselves before the Lord, and Satan also came with them." Job 1:6. It would seem reasonable to assume that since Lucifer had been evicted from Heaven, this meeting must have taken place somewhere else. At any rate, the implication is clear that he came uninvited. If, as some believe, the angels (or "sons of God" as some versions translate it) were representatives of inhabited worlds around the universe, then Satan obviously had elected himself the official delegate from Earth.

Behind the Scenes

The story, as it unfolds in Job 1 and 2, takes us behind the scenes of the great controversy between Christ and Satan and helps us see how this battle is being fought over each one of us. "Where have you come from?" God asked Satan.

"From roaming around Earth—from walking back and forth in it. That's my territory, you know. I'm in charge down there!"

"I see," God replied, then moved on to another question. "Have you met my servant Job yet? Have you noticed that there is no one else quite like him on Earth? He is a blameless man who worships me and stays away from evil."

Now, Job—according to the Bible—was not only a

very godly man but a very wealthy one as well. He
had—

> 7 sons and 3 daughters
> 7,000 sheep
> 3,000 camels
> 500 yoke of oxen
> 500 donkeys
> and a *lot* of servants.

"Do you really think Job worships you for nothing?"
Satan asked God. "That's no surprise. You never let
anything bad happen to him—and look at all you've
given him.

"But I'll guarantee you that if you take away all
those goodies, he will turn on you and curse you to
your face. This man has a bad case of cupboard love."

"Fine," God replied. "I'm confident I know what I
have in Job. You do whatever you want with what he
has—just don't lay a finger on him."

Satan wasted no time. He sped back to Earth and
called his Central Imperial Staff together. Quickly
briefing them, he issued specific assignments to his
immediate subordinates.

Database 3, File B-2120.729, Record 960
Imperial Order 55303.92
RE: Target 301-757-24464 ("Job")

Each of you has your individual orders. I don't need to
tell you how vital this operation is. The enemy himself
seems interested in making this a test case. Regrettably,
we are not free to attack the Target himself, but I've been
assured that we can go after anything that belongs to

him without any enemy interference.

Team 1 will whip up the Sabeans to steal the Target's oxen and donkeys and kill the servants watching the animals.

Team 2 will incinerate the Target's sheep and their shepherds.

Team 3 will use the Chaldeans to steal the Target's camels and kill the servants watching them.

Team 4 will see to it that the Target's children are all together for a party, then flatten the house with high winds and kill them all.

I will tolerate no holding back by any of you in this operation. Mercy is one of the greatest possible weaknesses, and any display of it will bring severe punishment and automatic demotion.

Each team should leave, however, one servant alive to carry the news to the Target, but other than that I want his possessions wiped out. Let the Target's wife live— she's already with us, and we can use her.

The goal of our operation, again, is twofold: (1) to prove that the Target worships the enemy only because of what the enemy gives him, and (2) to get the Target to blame the enemy for his losses and therefore turn away from him in anger and bitterness.

We will meet here in 24 hours for a post-operation review.

Lucifer,
Commander-in-chief, Imperial Forces
King of Earth
Most High God in Exile
UNIVERSAL EMPIRE

As the four breathless servants arrived in succession to break their bad news to Job, Lucifer was personally on hand—unseen as usual—to pressure Job into blaming God for his appalling misfortune.

Job's response?

He "got up and tore his robe and shaved his head. Then he fell to the ground in worship and said:

> Naked I came from my mother's womb,
>   and naked I will depart.
> The Lord gave and the Lord has taken away;
>   may the name of the Lord be praised.

"In all this," the Bible continues, "Job did not sin by charging God with wrongdoing." Job 1:20-22.

Amazing. Absolutely amazing! All Job's children are killed. He loses all his possessions. Does Job shake his fist toward Heaven and ask, "Why have You done this to me, Lord? Why did You let this happen?" No, he falls "to the ground in worship"!

True, Job does not see behind the scenes, as we who read his story centuries later are able to do. He *does* believe that his tragedies have come from God ("the Lord gave and *the Lord has taken away*"), but he does not sin "by charging God with wrongdoing."

Job is so well acquainted with God that he trusts Him implicitly. He has learned that anything his Friend in Heaven ever does has a good reason for it. He knows that whatever God has ever done in their friendship has been done out of nothing but love. He is unshakably certain that God is *on his side*.

Therefore, even though Job is hurting, even though he cannot imagine why God has let this happen, even though it seems out of character with how God has related to him before, he cannot turn his back on what he already knows of God. In his mind, it is settled. He will trust God no matter what happens—even if he can't answer the giant "Why?" that constantly repeats itself in his mind. If God has done this, Job is utterly convinced that He has a perfectly understandable and benevolent reason for it.

Round Two

Again the angels meet. Again Lucifer shows up uninvited. From God, the same question as before ("Where are you from?"). From Lucifer, the same answer.

"Have you noticed that there is still no one on Earth quite like my servant Job?" God asks. "In spite of all you have done, he is still a blameless man who worships me and stays away from evil."

"So what did you expect?" Satan retorts. "A man's possessions are one thing, but you haven't let me at Job himself. A man will do anything to save his own skin. Let me go after Job, and this time, I double-guarantee you that he will turn against you and curse you to your face!"

"Very well," God replies. "He's in your hands—but you cannot take his life."

Database 3, File B-2120.729, Record 961
Imperial Order 55303.93
RE: Target 301-757-24464 ("Job")

This Target is turning out to be a tougher nut to crack than we had thought. But now we have clearance to attack the Target himself. We can't kill him, but rest assured that by the time we're done with him, he'll wish he were dead. Your orders, as follows:

Team 1—Give the Target the most painful case of boils anyone has ever had. See to it that every square inch of his body is covered with them.

Team 2—Program his wife and then turn her loose on him.

Team 3—Send those three friends of his to "encourage" him.

Team 4—Stand guard. I'm not absolutely certain I can trust the enemy to let us get away with this without stepping in at some point.

Post-operation review in 24 hours.

Lucifer,
Commander-in-chief, Imperial Forces
King of Earth
Most High God in Exile
UNIVERSAL EMPIRE

Most of us know how painful one boil can be. But boils from the soles of the feet to the top of the head? Make no mistake about it, Job's suffering was intense. His agony was so great he undoubtedly wondered if he could cling to his sanity.

Others weren't much help, either. His wife's advice? "Curse God and die!" Job 2:9. Job's response? "Shall we accept good from God, and not trouble?" Verse 10.

The sympathy his three friends offered consisted of letting Job know that things like this just don't happen to good men—therefore Job must be guilty of some truly horrendous sin for God to punish him so severely.

Job Wins the Fight of Faith

But Job protested his innocence. And then, in words that spelled doom for Lucifer's efforts, he announced triumphantly through his pain, "Though He slay me, yet will I trust Him." Job 13:15, NKJV.

Even if God, for reasons I do not know and cannot understand, chooses to take my life, Job tells his friends, *I will still trust Him*!

On TV, things always turn out just rosy at the end of thirty or sixty minutes. It took a little longer in Job's case, but his story, too, had a happy ending. "The Lord made him prosperous again and gave him twice as much as he had before." Job 42:10.

Fourteen thousand sheep instead of 7,000; 6,000 camels instead of 3,000; 1,000 yoke of oxen and 1,000 donkeys instead of 500. True, God did not double the number of Job's children. He simply gave him another seven sons and three daughters. (But then, if God had given Job *twenty* new children, he might not have lived to be 140 years old!)

I believe that the story of Job has something very important to say for George and Joy Swift—and for little Lisa Steinberg. And I'd like to share with you what I believe Job's story has to say. But first, let's take a break—and I'll meet you again in the next chapter.

Chapter 9
Whodunit?

Typical Perry Mason plot: Villain plans perfect crime. Cleverly arranges evidence to implicate innocent man. Innocent man is arrested and brought to trial. Prosecutor builds apparently airtight case against innocent man based on overwhelming circumstantial evidence. Villain sits in courtroom reveling smugly in success of his frame-up. Perry Mason raises questions, introduces seemingly irrelevant evidence.

Finally, Perry Mason gets villain on witness stand. Asks relentless questions. Shows how his evidence reveals a strong motive. Tension builds. Finally Mason forces from villain a dramatic courtroom confession. Innocent man is visibly relieved as villain is handcuffed and led away. Judge vainly attempts to gavel the courtroom back to order.

Have you ever taken the rap for something you didn't do? Has anyone ever done something wrong and then pinned the blame on you? If so, you probably didn't like it one little bit. And if so, your sense of justice should be especially offended when you hear about the greatest frame-up ever attempted. Regrettably, the villain in this case has millions convinced that his crimes were—and still are—committed by someone else, someone entirely innocent.

When Satan—the greatest villain ever—attacked Job, who took the blame for it? The answer—as revealed in the Bible's book of Job—is clear. Let's rewind for a moment back to page 67.

"Do you really think Job worships you for nothing?" Satan asked God. "That's no surprise. You never let anything bad happen to him—and look at all you've given him."

Will the Real Villain Please Stand Up?

OK, freeze everything right there. What does Satan say next?

But stretch our YOUR hand and strike everything he has, and he will surely curse you to your face. Job 1:11, emphasis supplied.

Now notice carefully God's reply:

Very well, then, everything he has is in YOUR hands, but on the man himself do not lay a finger. Verse 12, emphasis supplied.

"YOU strike him, God," Satan says. "YOU reach our YOUR hand and hit him—and he'll curse you!"

But then God makes clear who is about to do the real dirty work. "Very well, he is in YOUR hands!"

Much to Satan's consternation, Job doesn't turn against God. So the devil returns to carry things one step further.

A man will give all he has for his own life. But

stretch out YOUR hand and strike his flesh and bones, and he will surely curse you to your face. Job 2:4, emphasis supplied.

And again, God makes clear who the real villain is:

Very well, then, he is in YOUR hands; but you must spare his life. Verse 6, emphasis supplied.

Then, just so none of us could miss it, the writer of the book of Job next says that "Satan went out from the presence of the Lord and afflicted Job with painful sores. Verse 7.

Who afflicted Job? Satan—not God!

Next notice the responses of those involved in this drama:

Job's wife:	"Curse God and die!"
Job's friends:	"God is punishing you for your terrible sins!"
Job:	"God gave—and He has taken away. Shall we accept good from Him, and not trouble?"

How to Make a Rebel

May I remind you again that Satan's Grand Strategy—his primary goal—is to convince us that God is our enemy. He will do anything—*anything at all*—to make it seem that God is against us. Because he knows that children don't rebel against parents when they are convinced their parents love them. But they *do* rebel against parents they are convinced *don't care*. Satan paints God with a character just like his own, in hopes of achieving a position just like God's!

Now, please consider carefully what I am going to say next. Unless you understand what is really going on behind the scenes in this great war between Christ and Satan—as revealed here in Job—the chances are very good that in time you will join Job's wife in blaming God for your troubles.

And if that happens, you are in great danger. Because it is impossible to continue loving someone you are convinced is hurting you, someone who cares nothing for you, someone who is against you.

Let's be fair. Job's wife *had* lost all of her ten children. She and her husband *had* lost everything they owned. And now he sat on an ash heap, covered with sores from head to foot. Her grief *is* understandable. But apparently Job's wife had not spent much time getting acquainted with God. If she had, she would have known who was her friend and who was her enemy.

What about Job's friends? They weren't the first or the last to decide that trouble is God's punishment for sin. Jesus and His disciples once encountered a man who had been blind from birth. "Rabbi," the disciples asked, "who sinned, this man or his parents, that he was born blind?" John 9:2. "Neither," Jesus replied.

Delayed Reaction

True, when we sin—when we break God's laws, whether moral or natural—the consequences are often immediate. Jump off a cliff, and you will do yourself some immediate and really heavy-duty damage. But sometimes the natural consequences of law-breaking are delayed. You don't get cancer from smoking one cigarette. But keep on smoking, and the statistics really get mean.

We also need to realize that sometimes we suffer through no fault of our own. Sometimes we suffer simply because we live in a sinful world. Sin has thrown a random, chaotic element into the perfect order God originally created. And you can count on two things being true about sin. Sin *always* brings suffering or pain—somebody gets hurt. And ultimately, sin *kills*. Always. At this point allow me to belabor the obvious. *God* didn't introduce sin into this world—*Satan* did.

We've noticed the reaction of Job's wife to their tragedy. And we know what his friends said. What about Job's reaction? After Satan's first attack, Job said, "The Lord gave and the Lord has taken away; may the name of the Lord be praised." Job 1:21.

"The Lord gave—and the Lord has taken away." Job was half right. The Lord had given. All that Job ever had came from God. But God was not the destroyer who took it all away. Because so often in the Bible God is described as doing that which He permits or does not prevent, it is very possible that Job viewed his tragedy in this light. If so, then when he said, "the Lord has taken [my possessions] away," he was really saying, "the Lord has *permitted* [my possessions] to be taken away."

In any event, the truly encouraging and amazing thing about Job's response is that he could conclude that God had either directly caused or permitted his troubles, yet still be unshaken in believing God to be his friend! He refused to charge God with wrongdoing. He refused to blame Him.

God once asked another Old Testament giant, Abraham, to slay his only son Isaac. Abraham couldn't understand why. It was unlike anything God had ever asked him to do. But Abraham knew God intimately. He knew from decades of personal experience that God never did anything that was not for his best good—*never*. He knew that God always did the most wise and loving thing he could do—*always*. Abraham's trust in God's love and wisdom was implicit and total.

"Even if He asks me to slay my own son, I will trust and obey him," Abraham decided. Job simply took the faith of Abraham one step further: "Even if He slays *me*, I will trust Him!"

Faith Under Fire

This kind of faith under fire—this kind of trust during trouble—is not natural. It is not normal. It is certainly not automatic. This incredible trust is the result of only one thing: having come to know God so well that confidence in His love, wisdom, and consistency is unshakable.

A few months ago we received a telephone call from Clyde and Janet—a young couple who were members of a church we had recently pastored. They had heard we would be returning to the area on business and invited us to stay with them.

Shortly before we were to leave on our trip, the phone rang again. Clyde had been in a serious accident as he drove home from work the evening before. Two teenaged young men were drag-racing side by side on a two-lane city street, when they came up suddenly behind Clyde's small pickup. One car zoomed past, but the other plowed into Clyde's pickup, which veered out of control. The pickup hit the street curb and flipped over on its top. Clyde suffered severe head injuries and was rushed unconscious to a hospital.

When we arrived at the airport, one of Clyde's

friends was waiting to rush us to his bedside. We prayed earnestly that God might miraculously heal him. We continued praying into the night and through the next day as Clyde fought for his life. But finally, we lost him. I had hoped on this trip to spend a happy meal around Clyde's table, enjoying the company of Clyde, Janet, and their two daughters. Instead, I preached his funeral.

And you have to be sure that the Big Question arose once again: "Why?"

The Good News in Job's Story

In the light of what we've learned from the book of Job, allow me to share with you what Job's story seems to me to say about that question. Let me share with you what I believe his story has to say to Janet and her family, to Joy and George Swift, to those who mourn for little Lisa Steinberg.

First, Job's story tells me—and them—that God is not the one who takes life. He is the one who gives it. God creates, Satan destroys, God restores. God is not our enemy, and Satan is not our friend.

Second, Job's story tells me that God does at times permit us to suffer—whether as a result of Satan's direct attacks, our own sinful choices, or simply because we live in a sin-filled world.

Third, Job's story tells me that we may not always know or understand why we have to suffer or grieve. Job apparently didn't know the reason for his suffering and tragedy. He was unaware that he was the immediate focus of the great war between Christ and Satan.

Fourth, Job's story tells me that being unable to answer the "Why?" does not give us an excuse to blame God for our troubles.

And fifth, Job's story tells me that when we know God well enough, we will have found Him to be so consistently wise and full of love in all His dealings with us, that our faith in that love cannot be shaken. We will be utterly sure that—even if we don't know the answer to our "Why?"—God does have reasons for permitting our trouble. And we will be unswerving in our belief that God's reasons are the wisest and most loving reasons possible. We will be convinced that if we could know what He knows, and love as He loves, we too would permit what He has permitted.

But, you may ask, Isn't it possible to glimpse at least a little of why God permits suffering? Yes, I believe it is. And I promise to share with you what I believe may be His primary reason in chapter 11.

Now, though, fast-forward with me through the long history of the great controversy to the day when its two mighty opponents come face to face in the blistering heat of a Palestinian desert.

Chapter 10
Duel in the Desert

Database 4, File R-4733.291, Record 62
[About A.D. 27]
Journal Entry 258.17

Finally we meet face to face, one on one. For over thirty years now I've watched him grow to be an adult human. About six weeks ago the deluded Target they call John the Baptizer actually baptized the enemy in the Jordan River. I stood unseen in the crowd and saw the spirit hover over his head in the form of a dove. I also heard the voice from Heaven claiming the enemy as his son.

The spirit, it would appear, has now made things easy for me. He has coerced the enemy into the desert, where this carpenter who pretends to be god seems bent on starving himself to death. He has been without food now for nearly a month and a half. He is very weak. He is vulnerable. I should be able to make quick work of him. But I'm taking no chances. I'll give it everything I've got. He will never know what hit him.

Only a few more steps . . .

As Jesus staggered the last few yards, His breath came in short, labored gasps. Just ahead, a massive, jagged boulder jutted abruptly out of the desert floor. Its cool shadow would offer at least some refuge from the shimmering heat of this parched wilderness inferno.

He fell heavily into the shaded yellow sand, then leaned back, bracing Himself against the crumbling wall of the great rock.

He was faint with a profound weakness. Even the smallest movement required an enormous, deliberate effort of will and body. Here in the shadow of this great slab of upturned limestone He closed His burning eyes in an effort to shut out the harsh reflection of the sun.

But He could not shut out the hunger.

After forty days of intimate communion with the Father, oblivious to all else, hunger had returned with a desperate intensity. It seemed that every cell of His body cried out for food with the demanding urgency of a drowning man for air. The hunger he felt was constant, wracking, all-consuming. But the Father would provide. When the time was right, He would provide.

A sudden sharp clattering of dry desert stones shattered the silence. As Jesus wearily opened His eyes, He saw someone emerging from behind the clump of scrubby bushes a few yards away. Momentarily, a tall being of majestic and commanding appearance stood before Him. Light seemed to radiate from his clothing. An angel sent from the Father to bring food and strength?

"I have come to you directly from the Father's side," the visitor announced, as if reading His thoughts. "He has given me a message for you. He says that you are to end your fast. You have passed His test of obedience, and He is very pleased with you. You haven't tried to provide for yourself—you have waited for Him to provide for you."

Just Testing

The tall stranger peered into the distance, as if absorbed in trying to recall something.

"You undoubtedly remember reading," he continued, "about what happened with Abraham and Isaac. The Father only wanted to see if Abraham was really willing to give up his son—He never intended that Abraham actually go through with it. And do you remember how, at the last moment, the Father sent His angel to stay Abraham's hand?

"Well," the visitor went on, "I was that angel. And now I've been sent to you with the same message I gave Abraham. The Father wanted to see if you would be willing to set your feet in the path of suffering and death—but it certainly will not be necessary for you actually to walk in it. Your simple willingness is all that He asks. So now you're free to go ahead and provide for yourself.

"Do you see those stones lying there next to your feet? They are about the shape of loaves of bread, right? So I would suggest that if you are the Son of God, you just make those stones into bread and end your fast."

Already Jesus had recognized His visitor as the great enemy, Satan—the fallen Lucifer. He knew him, not by his appearance, but by his words. Subtle words of thinly veiled doubt. *"If you are the Son of God."* Shouldn't the Father's angel be able to find and recognize Him without question?

But Lucifer flattered himself that Jesus had not yet seen through his assumed identity. Stepping closer to Jesus, he appeared to be studying Him intently.

"As I've said, you're free to make food for yourself now—that is, if indeed you really are the Son of God. Now that I've had a closer look at you, I'm beginning to wonder about that.

"I notice that your clothes are torn and rumpled, you're thin as a rail, and you look wasted. Going by how you look, it would be stretching it even to see you as one of the lowest angels of Heaven—much less as their Commander."

With great difficulty, Jesus moved a few inches to stay within the shifting shadow of the overhanging rock, but He said nothing as His expressionless eyes followed His now pacing tormenter.

"Aha!" the devil exclaimed as he suddenly stopped and wheeled to face Jesus once again. "I think I may know now who you really are, after all. Some time ago, as you well know, one of the highest angels of Heaven was thrown out and exiled here on Earth. And if you ask me, I'd put money on it that you are that angel. I mean, can you really picture the Son of God looking like you do? Wouldn't it be reasonable to assume that the King of the Universe would look like I do—only better, since I'm just an angel?

"Now, as the Father's angel, I should let you know that He has given me the right to require that you prove who you think you are. Given how you look, it is only fair to ask that you supply us with some clear evidence that you really are the Son. If you are the Son, then of course you have the same power as the Father. So why not prove it and remove all doubt by making these stones into bread?"

The Voice at Jordan

Jesus sat in silence, glancing languidly at the round stones lying scattered upon the sand at His feet. He knew that He had no proof that He was really the Son of God. He had to take it on pure faith—faith in the deepening convictions within Him as He had grown up searching the prophecies of the coming Messiah—and faith especially in the Voice that had confirmed His divinity there on the sloping Jordan riverbank.

A new wave of almost overpowering hunger seized Him, and it felt as if His entire body trembled in utter weakness.

"Do you see this?" the taunting prince of demons asked, drawing something from a fold in his brilliant robe. "As you can see, this is a loaf of fresh bread. And if you are the Son of God, you can easily make as much of it as you want!"

Walking over to Jesus, Satan seated himself directly in front of his haggard opponent. Then, tearing off a large piece of the bread, he slowly ate it with obvious satisfaction, savoring every morsel. The air Jesus breathed was soon filled with the enticing aroma of freshly baked bread.

Jesus closed His eyes, pleading earnestly in urgent prayer to the Father for more than human power to resist. The perspiration of a man under great stress tracked wet pathways down His gaunt face.

Satan stood and gestured broadly at the empty wasteland surrounding them.

"Do you honestly believe that God would leave His own Son out here in this forsaken place, surrounded by wild animals, and starving to death? Does that make any sense at all? Do you really believe that a Father of love could let this happen to His own Son, and just stand by and do nothing?

"You believe that you are the Father's Son. Fine— but are you *sure*? Are you absolutely certain? How do you know? What evidence do you have? I say that every reasonable evidence says that either you are pathetically deluded, or else you are a blasphemous imposter. Believe me, I know perhaps better than anyone else that the Father loves His Son far too much ever to allow Him to be found in the predicament you're in.

"So you see, God needs to know, I need to know, and you need to know if you really are who you seem to think you are. So go ahead and prove it. Make yourself some bread, if you can—and then we'll all know for sure."

"It Is Written!"

Jesus began to move. Slowly, laboriously, He struggled to His feet. Once standing, He seemed to draw from some hidden source of strength, and there was a resonant authority in His voice as He fastened His penetrating eyes upon His sadistic enemy and spoke to him for the first time.

"It is written," He responded in clear tones that cut through the desert stillness, " 'Man does not live on bread alone, but on every word that comes from the mouth of God.' "

For a long moment the devil stood—stunned, silenced, beaten. Then he leaned down slowly, picked up his unfinished loaf of bread, and walked to the far side of the giant boulder where Jesus could not see him. Trembling in fury, he raised the partially eaten bread into the air and, with all the force of his pent-up rage, threw it as far as he could throw it.

A sudden shadow darkened the hot sand at Jesus' feet.

Only a few minutes earlier, His great tormenter had walked out of His sight to the far side of the gigantic desert boulder against which He rested. Now this moving shadow signaled his return.

Still wearing the brilliant robes of an angel, and still believing that Jesus might not have seen through his guise, Satan stood squarely in front of the emaciated form on the sand at his feet.

Without a word, he swiftly bent and swept Jesus up in his muscular arms. Jesus offered no resistance. There was no struggle. In His great weakness, He was no match for this powerful fallen angel. And if the Father did not intervene to free Him, Jesus would not try to free Himself.

The pleasant rush of cool wind over His feverish body—the sensation of traveling at great speed—and suddenly Jesus found Himself standing next to His uninvited adversary atop the highest pinnacle of the temple in Jerusalem.

"You have responded as you should have back there in the desert," He heard Satan saying approvingly. "As you can see, the Father has asked me to test thoroughly your dependence on Him. In view of what is ahead of you, He needed to find out early on if you would trust Him even under great pressure. I am personally amazed and very pleased at how well you have passed the Father's test so far."

Only with the greatest effort did Jesus remain calm as He listened to the transparent pretentiousness and undisguised flattery of the devil's blasphemous charade.

"The Father asks only one more proof of your absolute trust in Him," the masquerading arch-rebel continued. "If you are indeed the Son of God, it is necessary for you to prove that by jumping off from this pinnacle right now."

Jesus looked down from the dizzy height where He

stood to the city street far, far below.

"Go ahead and jump," Satan urged. "After all, if you are the Son of God, you don't have anything to fear. Do you think the Father would ever permit any harm to come to His Son? That's totally unthinkable!

"And, of course, you and I both know what has been written: 'He will command his angels concerning you, and they will lift you up in their hands, so that you will not strike your foot against a stone.'

"So you have the Father's word in writing. What could there possibly be to worry about?" The devil paused only a moment before continuing. "Unless, of course, you are not really the Son of God after all. Then you would have good reason to be afraid. Could that be the reason you are hesitating? You're not absolutely certain that you really are God's Son, are you? Well, why not prove it—jump, and let's all find out!"

Jesus looked down at the street; then slowly His gaze traveled over the whole city beneath Him. For several moments He seemed absorbed in thought. Then His eyes met the eyes of His waiting tempter.

"If you know so well what the Father has said," He answered, "then surely you know that these words also stand written: 'Do not put the Lord your God to the test.' "

Turning his back to Jesus, Satan clenched his teeth and his fists and in furious puzzlement wondered how any man so weak could be so strong.

Act III

His eyes blazed with searing fire.

The act was over. The mask was off. The pretense was ended. Satan stood facing Jesus on the high mountaintop to which he had just carried Him.

"All right. No more games. You know who I am, and

I know who you are. I am the god of this world, and you—you are Jesus!" The prince of rebels visibly shuddered as he spat out the name of his hated adversary.

"Whatever else you may think, let's get one thing clear. *This world is mine!*" The devil was shouting now. "It's *mine*—do you understand? MINE! I'm in charge of it all. Wherever it is that you may think you're god, on this Earth I am. Clear enough? These people rejected you a long time ago and chose me instead."

With a sweeping arc of his arm, Satan gestured toward the valleys which lay below them in every direction. "Take a look," he commanded icily—"take a good look."

In a spectacular panoramic procession, the kingdoms of the world, past and present, appeared before Jesus in all their glory. Scene after scene of unsurpassed beauty and prosperity came into view. Cities, palaces, fields, and vineyards basked in the sunlight.

As Jesus viewed the entrancing spectacle before Him, the devil spoke again. "All of this is mine. You want it back, and that's why you're here. And I know that you are planning to try to get it back. But to get it back it's going to cost you. You're going to have to suffer. You'll have to go through the worst suffering and pain and agony you can imagine. And finally you will die like a dumb animal—and for what? This world and everyone in it will still be mine, and you will have thrown away your life for nothing.

"But listen to me. You don't have to suffer. You don't have to die. Do you see all these kingdoms of mine? Have you seen all the people? You can have them all right now, and I'll turn over the rulership of the whole world to you again, if you'll do just one simple thing for me—just one small favor.

"All you need to do is admit that I am the god of this world by just quickly kneeling here in front of me for a moment—and then you can have it all. No one else is around but you and me. No one would ever see you. No one would ever know but the two of us. No one would ever . . ."

Jesus, unable to tolerate the horrendous suggestions of the chief of demons a moment longer, stopped him in midsentence.

"Away from me, Satan!" He commanded in words of unmistakably divine authority that shook the mountaintop. "For it is written: 'Worship the Lord your God, and serve him *only*.' "

Satan was powerless to resist the command of the Earth's real King. Consumed with humiliation, frustration, and rage, he turned and retreated swiftly down the hillside, disappearing into the shadows cast by the sinking afternoon sun.

Another Mountain

He had lost the battle. But he promised himself that he would yet win the war. This would not be the last mountaintop where the two of them would meet. Already his thoughts raced ahead to another mountain.

A mountain just outside Jerusalem. A mountain already cluttered with the crosses of executed criminals. A mountain in great need, he decided, of at least one more cross.

Chapter 11
Duel on the Mountain

In his book *Beyond Knoche's Law*,* pastor-author-artist-musician Keith Knoche—in his consummately droll style—tells of his run-in with Rocko Marconi.

Rocko was the terror of Keith's college campus—built like an earthmover, familiar with karate and tae-kwon-do, and fond of saying things like, "My mouth don't write no checks my body can't cash!"

One Saturday night Keith took Carmelita Malblotto to the lyceum travelogue, only to discover to his horror that Carmelita was Rocko's girlfriend. Glancing over his shoulder, Keith spied Rocko's roommate, Lionel Snuglaster, two rows back. Lionel's face wore a fiend-ish grin, and suddenly Keith knew he was doomed.

Monday morning as Keith sat tying his tennis shoelaces in the gym locker room, a huge viselike hand clamped onto his shoulder. Rocko.

"My roommate Lionel tells me you were out with Carmelita last Saturday night. Is that true?"

I nodded, my chin quivering out of control.

"I wish you hadn't done that. Now I have to teach

---

*Beyond Knoche's Law, by Keith Knoche. Copyright 1983 by Pacific Press Publishing Association, Boise, Idaho.

you a lesson," he said, pulling me up two feet off the concrete by my collar.

The best defense is a good offense, someone has said, so I decided to try to intimidate him by a show of brute strength. Springing loose, I poised ready to strike. Holding my hands in karate fashion, I said, "Rocko, I am required by law to warn you that my hands are lethal weapons registered with the U.S. government and that should you try to start anything I would be—"

Before I could finish my sentence the fight began. Thrusting my nose firmly between his teeth, I threw him to the ground heavily on top of me. I pummelled his knee with my stomach and climaxed the bout by giving him a crushing blow on his fist with my chin. Lights out.—*Beyond Knoche's Law*, pp. 32, 33.

Keith's story contains the one nearly indispensable element of good narrative writing: conflict. A story may have colorful characterization, a strong plot, scintillating dialogue—but unless it has conflict, it will lie there on the page like so much soggy mush.

Two heavyweight boxers face off in the ring.
Two NFL teams square off on the gridiron.
Two nuclear nations play chicken with their missiles.
Two presidential nominees race for the White House.

Conflict. Competition. Confrontation.

Cops and robbers.
Cowboys and Indians.
Hatfields and McCoys.
Cats and dogs.

Conflict can be played out small-scale—as in a

"friendly" game of Monopoly. Or it can be played out large-scale—as in all-out world war. But even a world war is small potatoes when placed in the context of the great conflict we've been discussing in this book. No other conflict will ever match it for magnitude, for deadly intensity, for its unimaginably high stakes.

The Decisive Battle

This great conflict of the ages, initiated by Satan against his Creator, is the overarching war behind all wars. And just as in nearly every major war of Earth, one decisive battle has been fought, so in this titanic struggle a pivotal battle was fought.

The deciding battle took place just short of 2000 years ago now, on a lonely hilltop just outside Jerusalem. There on Mount Calvary, the two mighty opponents faced off, knowing that one of them would win and the other would lose.

> You see, Calvary was a battlefield. It was the scene of the most crucial, the most critical, the most decisive showdown in the controversy between Christ and Satan—a controversy that began in heaven and today is moving toward its final windup. It is only in the setting of that controversy that we can begin to comprehend what really happened at Calvary. In fact, to understand that controversy is to understand the Bible. For the Bible is the story of that ongoing conflict—the story of God's plan to save men, and Satan's attempt to thwart it.—*The Cry of a Lonely Planet*, p. 137.*

---

* *The Cry of a Lonely Planet*, by George E. Vandeman. Copyright 1983 by Pacific Press Publishing Association, Boise, Idaho.

Nearly everyone knows the basic facts of the story of Calvary—how Jesus was crucified between two thieves, how He died "to save us from our sins," how He was buried in Joseph's new tomb and returned to life on the third day.

But to really appreciate and understand the cross, we must get beyond historical fact. What *really* happened at Calvary? Why did Jesus die? What did He accomplish by dying on the cross?

Jesus died to prove that Satan's charges against God's character were false. For centuries, Satan had harped away on the idea that God did not care about human beings—that He was, in fact, the sworn enemy of mankind. But Calvary proved just how much God *did* care! On the cross it became clear that God loved His created beings more than His own life.

Jesus died to unmask Satan's real character before the universe. When Satan put his own Creator on the cross and tortured and murdered Him, he destroyed whatever trace of sympathy that may have remained for his cause anywhere in the universe. His claims for the superiority of his self-centered approach to government were exposed for the lies they were.

Jesus died to reconcile us to the Father. When the human race sinned, it became estranged from God—hostile toward Him. But in giving His Son to die on the cross, God took the initiative to heal the broken relationship—to reconcile us to Himself. See 2 Corinthians 5:19.

And how does the cross bring reconciliation? As it begins to dawn on us what Christ really did for us there—how He took the ultimate consequences of all our sins—how He unhesitatingly threw away His own life that we might live—how He made it possible for us once more to stand before God as if we had never sinned—as we see this amazing outpouring of love, we lose all appetite for our foolish rebellion and return gladly to our Father's arms.

Jesus died as us. And what does that mean? It means that just as we were all included in Adam when he sinned, and therefore were doomed to reap the inevitable consequences of sin, just so through God we were also included in Christ—who reaped those deadly consequences for us. As the second Adam—the new head of the human race—Christ is sinless and guiltless before God. And unless we refuse to permit God to include us in Christ, we too stand perfect before our Father. But only as we are *in Christ.*

Jesus died to prove that His law could not be changed. From the beginning of the great controversy, Satan had attacked God's eternal law. In Heaven, as Lucifer, he had challenged God's law of love. And God's law, which is simply a perfect transcript of His own character of love, cannot be broken without penalty.

Once Lucifer himself broke God's law, he realized he would inevitably reap the natural consequence of his own rebellious choice—death. Therefore he lobbied hard to persuade God to set aside His law in just this one case.

But God could not set aside His law without bringing in chaos. The whole foundation of happiness for the universe would crumble. Seeing that God would not set aside the law for him, Lucifer declared war on it, calling it unfair, arbitrary, and impossible to keep.

And when Adam and Eve joined him in disobedience, this seemed to prove the devil's point that the law could not be kept.

If God could have set His law aside, or changed it, then no penalty or consequences would follow breaking it. And if no one needed to reap that penalty of death, Christ did not need to die on the cross. Christ's death on Calvary *proved* that the law could not be changed—that someone had to reap its inevitable consequences.

Jesus died to sin-proof the universe. Once this great controversy—this great experiment in rebellion—is over, sin will never rise up again. See Nahum 1:9. Why? Will God take away our free will? Will He program us like so many computers so that we have no choice but to worship Him and keep His law?

No, God has chosen instead to immunize us against sin. You see, Calvary proves to us once and for all that *sin kills!* Sin *always* kills. Death is its inescapable consequence. And as we see what happened to Jesus when He took the consequences of our own sins, we will come to hate sin with an ever-deepening passion.

Andy Skips the Watermelon

Long tables, groaning under the weight of good food, seemed to stretch all the way to the horizon. The potluck bounty of the annual church picnic was a feast for the eyes as well as the palate.

Bob and Andy made their way together down one side of the line, loading their plates high with a multitude of samples from the impossibly large selection available.

After finishing their first round, the two men returned to the tables for seconds.

"Say, check out that watermelon!" Bob remarked. "I do believe I'll have myself a big slice. How about you?"

"No way!" Andy replied. "I don't eat watermelon."

"You what?" Bob answered in surprise. "What do you mean, 'you don't eat watermelon'? *Everybody* eats watermelon."

"Well, I don't," Andy said. "Go ahead and grab your slice, and we'll go sit back down under that tree. And then I'll tell you why I don't eat watermelon."

"OK—so what do you have against watermelon?" Bob asked when they were back in the shade.

"Well, you see, when I was just a kid, we lived next to a mean old farmer who grew watermelons. And every now and then, when the melons would start to get ripe, some of my neighbor friends and I would sneak over at night through the barbed-wire fence into his watermelon patch and have ourselves a real feast. We wouldn't even bother to eat the whole watermelon. We'd just split one open and eat just the heart with no seeds in it. We could wipe out a lot of melons in one night.

"One night we headed over to the watermelon patch again. We thumped melons until we found one we thought was ripe; then we got ready to cut it open. But none of us had remembered to bring our pocket knives. So we just made do. We took the melon over and split it over the top of one of the tree stumps that were scattered around the field.

"And then—the stump *moved*!

"Just then the moon came out from behind the clouds, and we saw the old farmer sitting there with watermelon juice and seeds running down his face—and a big shotgun in his lap!

" 'Good evening, boys!' he said. 'I see you like watermelons.'

" 'Uh—no, not really,' I told him. 'In fact, we were just leaving.'

" 'Oh, come now, boys,' the farmer protested. 'Now that you've opened it, you might as well eat it.' And we could see that the barrel of the shotgun was now pointing right at us.

"Somehow, we finished the watermelon, even though we had somehow lost our appetites. Then we got up to go.

" 'Please, boys. Don't leave now. I wouldn't want word to get around that I'm stingy with my watermelons. Please have another.'

"Well, somehow we choked down another one. And another. The old farmer kept his shotgun on us until we had eaten so much watermelon that we *looked* like watermelons—full and round and green. Somehow, we all staggered home, and we never set foot in the watermelon patch again. And ever since then, it's all I can do to even look at a watermelon."

Sick of Sin

When you've had enough—too much—of something, you get sick of it. And once we have finally had enough of sin, we will loathe it. We'll be nauseated by it. We'll never want to touch it again.

If we still enjoy sin, maybe we haven't had enough of it yet. Maybe after we see enough pain and grief and death, we'll lose our appetite for it. Maybe once we stand at the foot of the cross long enough to understand that sin—our sin—killed our innocent Creator, maybe then it won't seem so attractive.

If the universe is ever going to be sin-proof and safe, it must be populated only with those who find sin so repulsive they would rather die than to sin again. And maybe, my friend, just maybe, that helps explain why

God doesn't always shield us from the consequences of sin. If He did, we would never connect sin with its natural consequences. We would never be able to weigh sin's admitted temporary pleasure against its inevitable price.

If God is to make us safe to save, He must permit us to taste enough of sin's gall to make us abhor it. He must let us suffer enough of its pain that we will never ever be tempted to experiment with it again.

And if, for me, that means that God must force Himself not to step in and prevent the suffering or death of someone I love, then may I accept that pain as the pain of immunization.

Every time I attend another funeral or watch an innocent child racked by fever or hear of the savagery and suffering plaguing this world, I become just a bit more willing—even eager—to let God do whatever it takes to make me hate sin.

And when I see that the very sins that I have most enjoyed have killed my greatest Friend, I am grieved and disgusted. How can any sin be worth the life of God? Maybe if I kept that vision of my dying Creator more clearly and constantly in mind, I would not sin so readily—so almost casually.

Unlike Andy, I still eat watermelon. And I still sin. But one of those indulgences I want desperately to quit. And you?

Chapter 12
Confessions of a News Junkie

It all started with Dick and Jane and Spot and Puff. Once I learned to read, I was hooked. And today my reading addiction borders on an obsession. If I were ever banished to a desert island with nothing to read, I'd go stark raving bananas.

What's really frightening is that I think I've passed on my disease to my four kids. One of my daughters not only reads everything in sight—she *speedreads* it. If I had to buy enough printed matter to support her habit, I'd be bankrupt in a week.

Fortunately, though, my daughter is like me. Once we've vacuumed up all the books and magazines around, we'll read *anything*. I read cereal boxes, the Yellow Pages, junk mail, and the instructions on the kitty litter bag. When I'm stuck in a waiting room, the inevitable stack of year-old knitting magazines suits me fine.

My addiction is at its worst when it comes to news. Without my daily news fix, I get the shakes. Every now and then I'll get so immersed in some pressing project that I don't have time for anything else. But eventually when I come up for air, panic strikes with the realization that it's been days since I've been in touch with What's Going On.

So in a frantic frenzy, I'll commence to pork out on *Time*, *Newsweek*, *U.S. News*, *U.S.A. Today*, Brokaw, Rather, Jennings, CNN, and my state and local newspapers. I just keep wolfing down megadoses of news till the shaking stops. My friends want me to join Newsaholics Anonymous—and maybe I should.

One thing I've learned from my affliction is that the daily news is a mixed bag of good and bad—and mostly bad. It sort of reminds me of the dumb little story some of us thought was so hilarious back in grade school:

"I went flying today."

"Oh? That's good!"

"No, it's bad—because the engine quit."

"I see. Well, that's bad."

"No, it's good—because luckily I had a parachute and jumped out."

"That's good!"

"No, it's bad—because the parachute wouldn't open."

"That's bad."

"No, it's good—because there was a huge haystack down below."

"That's good."

"No, it's bad—because there was a pitchfork in the haystack pointing straight up."

"That's bad."

"No, it's good—because I missed the pitchfork."

"That's good."

"No, it's bad—because *I missed the haystack too*!"

Now, as the familiar question goes, which do you want first—the good news or the bad news? Because we are going to take a look at both in this chapter.

OK—let's get the bad news out of the way, then finish with the good news. And I promise you—the good news is very good indeed.

Ever since the devil took over down here, the news has been mostly bad. And today, leaving behind the 1980s and racing on through the 1990s to the year 2000, we see evidence that the devil is working harder than ever to stir up trouble on our tired old planet. It's like John said in the Bible—"The devil had gone down to you! He is filled with fury, because he knows that his time is short." Revelation 12:12.

So far in this short book, we've looked only backward in time. We began by focusing on the beginning of the great cosmic war between Christ and Satan. Then we traced it down through Old Testament times and on to the pivotal confrontation between the two great opponents at Calvary.

In the nearly 2,000 years since the cross, the battle has raged on. (The question of *why* the war continues, even though it has already been won at the cross, will be explored in the next chapter.) Satan has not let up even a moment in his attacks on God's character and on God's people.

But today we are living down near the end of the long, terrible war. And Satan, sensing that his time is running out, is pulling out all the stops to attack, harass, and destroy the citizens of Earth. Though he is a mastermind at overall strategy, be sure that his planning is also detailed enough that he has a personalized strategy that applies just to you—and to me.

Database 5, File C-49088.30, Record 354
[Late 1980s]
Strategy Directive 3099.41
RE: Target-Enemy Relationships

Once again, our primary objective for Targets is to convince them that our enemy is also their enemy. Therefore our total effort must focus on preventing any of them from getting to know him. No sooner do they get acquainted with him than they fall under the spell of his so-called love.

Having once felt the force of this enemy delusion ourselves, we know how powerful it is. Those most under its influence not only come to trust the enemy, they also become increasingly difficult for us to win over.

I remind you that every weapon and tactic at our disposal must be brought to bear on those Targets who show signs of attempting to form a relationship with the enemy. Do not be overly concerned with Targets who simply go through all the supposedly correct religious motions, but who privately make no attempt to communicate regularly with the enemy. But at any time we encounter Targets praying to the enemy or trying to learn more about him through reading the book of lies, we must spare no effort to interrupt such communication.

When they communicate with the enemy, they get to know him. When they know him well enough, they trust him. When they trust him, they love him. And when they love him enough, we've lost them.

Use our successful and proven methods of interrupting Target-enemy communication:

1. *Busyness.* Keep the lives of Targets so full of other things that they have no time for communicating with the enemy.

2. *Diversion.* Shift their attention away to entertainment, leisure pursuits, money-making, or anything else—just so long as it becomes a higher priority than getting to know the enemy.

3. *Discouragement.* Perhaps the most effective

weapon in our arsenal. Convince Targets that pursuing a "spiritual" life is impossibly difficult, that it doesn't work, that their sins are proof that they are failures.

4. *Trouble*. Hit them hard and then get them to blame the enemy for their troubles. Convince them that if the enemy really loved them, he would not let these things happen to them.

Lucifer,
Commander-in-chief, Imperial Forces
King of Earth
Most High God in Exile
UNIVERSAL EMPIRE

Enough, for now, of the bad news. Because much good news awaits us. The Bible even contains a word which means "good news." That word is *gospel*. "This *gospel* of the kingdom," Matthew wrote, "will be preached in the whole world as a testimony to all nations, and then the end will come." Matthew 24:14, emphasis supplied.

And what is the good news? The good news includes everything that God has been doing since Lucifer's rebellion to get rid of sin. God is a God of love, but there is one thing He hates—and that is sin. He hates it because it destroys everything it touches. He hates it because it brings death to those He created and loves.

Sin is bad news. The gospel is good news. Sin is the problem. The gospel is God's solution. Sin destroys. The gospel restores.

Penalty, Power, Presence

The problem of sin has three parts—its *penalty*, its *power*, and its *presence*. And the good news, the gospel, includes what God does about each of those three parts of the sin problem.

For the balance of this chapter, I'd like to consider what God has already done about sin's penalty. Then in the chapters ahead, we'll look at how He deals with sin's power and presence.

Sin, the Bible clearly says, carries its own built-in penalty. The natural, inevitable consequence of sin is death: "The wages of sin is death." Romans 6:23.

Death is not a punishment God inflicts on those who break His rules—His Law. Death is the automatic result of breaking the laws of God.

Imagine for a moment that you're an astronaut. You're outside your spaceship taking pictures, when the insane urge comes over you to remove your helmet. We all know what will happen to you if you give in to that senseless notion. You will die. It is a natural law that man cannot live without oxygen.

If you do remove your helmet and you die, did God kill you? Is death His punishment for breaking His natural law? (And, by the way, isn't the purpose of punishment to educate—to help a person learn to associate negative behavior with unpleasant consequences? If so, how can you "learn" anything to help you in making your future choices, if you're dead?)

God does not kill you for disconnecting your oxygen supply. Death is the natural consequence of your own unwise choice. And the law of nature that says you will die without oxygen is also not your enemy. This law does not kill you—it *warns* you! It's on your side. It's there to protect you—not to restrict you. If God's laws restrict us at all, they restrict us from hurting ourselves.

And that is the purpose of all of God's laws— natural and moral. When we live within His laws, we are happy, healthy, and holy. But when we ignore them, we do great damage to ourselves.

Artificial Life Support

Just as we cannot continue to live if we cut ourselves off from oxygen, we cannot continue to live if we cut ourselves off from God. He is the Source of all life. And when Adam and Eve chose to sin, they cut themselves off from the Source of life. They would have died immediately if God had not instantly stepped in and placed them on artificial life support. And the human race—the descendents of Adam and Eve—have been on artificial life support ever since.

Why? Because God wanted to heal the broken relationship between Him and His creatures that resulted from their selfish choice. He wanted to demonstrate fully to them the sure results of choosing sin in contrast with choosing the way of love. He wanted them to be able—after seeing the sure results of both choices—to choose again. And He wanted time to demonstrate that love is far superior to selfishness.

Sin's ultimte penalty—its natural consequence—is death. And by death, the Bible means eternal death. Death that is everlasting oblivion. Death that says goodbye to life forever.

One of the many tragic results of sin is that we grow old, wear out, and die. But this death—if we die in Christ—is just a temporary rest in the grave until the resurrection day. It is not that "second death" the Bible talks about (see Revelation 20:14) from which there will never be a resurrection.

And when Adam, the head of the human race, sinned, the second death passed over all of us. "Sin entered the world through one man," Paul wrote, "and death through sin, and in this way death came to all men, because all sinned." Romans 5:12.

You see, all of us were in Adam there in Eden. God considered the whole human race to be in him. Therefore whatever happened to Adam happened to us all. Just as the first mountain climber on a rope may fall and take all the others down the precipice with him, when Adam fell, he took us all down with him. So when Adam came under the power of death, we all did.

Biologically speaking, of course, we were all quite definitely "in Adam" in Eden. The life that was in Adam has been passed on through countless generations, in one unbroken stream, to you and to me. If you have any doubts that you were in Adam there in Eden, consider where you would be just now if he had died with no children!

But in a far broader sense than just biology, in God's reckoning we have all been included in Adam. See 1 Corinthians 1:30. So when it comes to sin's consequences, God deals with this problem not just individually, but corporately.

What Adam did when he sinned, you see, affected us all. We all—and each—were doomed to reap the natural consequences of Adam's choice. Therefore whatever God did to solve the problem also had to affect us all.

Listen to the good news: "Just as the result of one trespass [sin] was condemnation [the death penalty] for all men, so also the result of one act of righteousness was justification that brings life for all men." Romans 5:18.

Life for all men! If you are under a death sentence, and that sentence is lifted, may I suggest to you that

that is good news? And that is precisely what has happened.

Adam II

How? Through the life and death of a *second Adam*. " 'The first man Adam became a living being'; the last Adam, a life-giving spirit. . . . The first man was of the dust of the earth, the second man from heaven. As was the earthly man, so are those who are of the earth; and as is the man from heaven, so also are those who are of heaven." 1 Corinthians 15:45-48.

Did you catch that last sentence? Whatever goes for the earthly man (Adam) goes for us. But, whatever goes for the man from heaven (Jesus) *also* goes for us!

It would not have been fair if, after Adam sinned, God had simply suspended the natural penalty of sin. And He didn't. The penalty would still have to follow the sin. And it did. But instead of falling on us, God placed it on His own Son, Jesus Christ, as the *new* head of the human race. And on the cross, Jesus reaped in full not only the penalty of Adam's sin, which separated a whole race from God, but the penalty also of all the countless sins that would follow that first one.

On the cross, Jesus died as the new head of the human race. And God, in His reckoning, has included every one of us in Jesus. So unless we *reject* the life that Jesus now offers us, we once again have the right to eternal life. We are forgiven. We are free. We are reconciled to the Father.

But even after hearing such good news, we may choose to cling to our selfishness and reject what Jesus has provided for us at such an enormous cost to Himself. The good news about how God solves the problem of sin's penalty is that He bears it

Himself as the head of our race. And what an unthinkable tragedy it would be if we should choose to live outside of Christ—and thus reject His pardon.

Rejected Pardon

Several years ago, a southern California newspaper carried the following article:

A young man who lived in the Western states had never done anything [criminally] wrong. But one day while playing a game of cards he lost his temper. Picking up a revolver, he shot and killed his opponent. He was arrested, tried, and sentenced to hang.

Because of the wonderful life he had previously lived, his relatives and friends got up a petition for him. It seemed as though everyone wanted to sign it. Before long other towns and villages had heard about it, and people all over the state eagerly signed.

At last it was taken to the governor, who happened to be a Christian, and tears came to his eyes as he looked at the large baskets filled with petitions. He decided to pardon the young man; so, writing out a pardon, he put it in his pocket, then, dressed in the garb of a clergyman, he made his way to the prison.

As the governor approached the death cell the young man sprang to the bars: "Get out of here," he cried. "I don't want to see you. I have had enough religion at home. Seven of your kind have visited me already."

"But," interrupted the governor, "wait a moment, young man; I have something for you. Let me talk to you."

"Listen," exclaimed the young man in anger. "If you don't get out of here at once, I'll call the guard and have you put out."

"But, young man," continued the governor, "I have news for you—the very best. Won't you let me tell you about it?"

"You heard what I said," replied the young man, "and if you don't leave immediately, I'll call the warden."

"Very well," replied the governor, and with a sad heart he turned and left.

In a few moments the warden approached. "Well, young man," he said, "I see you had a visit from the governor."

"What!" cried the man. "Was that man dressed in the garb of a clergyman the governor?"

"He was," replied the warden, "and he had a pardon in his pocket for you, but you would not listen to him."

"Get me pen, ink, and paper," urged the young man. And sitting down, he wrote, "Dear Governor: I owe you an apology. I am sorry for the way I treated you. . . ."

The governor received the letter, turned it over, and wrote on the back, "No longer interested in this case."

The day came for the young man to die. "Is there anything you want to say before you die?" he was asked.

"Yes," he answered, "tell the young men of America that I am not dying for my crime—I am not dying because I am a murderer. The governor pardoned me. I could have lived. Tell them," he continued, "that I am dying because I did not accept the governor's pardon."—*The Arlington Times*, August 26, 1954.

Not one of us will be lost because of our sins. Jesus has taken the penalty for them all at the cross. If any of us are finally lost, it will be because we have rejected Christ's pardon. May that never be my decision—or yours!

Chapter 13
Why the War Isn't Over

Several years ago, back when Walter Cronkite was still the anchorman of the CBS Evening News on television, I wrote a little parable for *Insight* magazine called "The Good News Fight." The parable attempts to illustrate how Christians sometimes get very upset with one another over just what the good news includes:

Halfway through his nightly recital of the world's hang-ups, Walter Cronkite's benign countenance suddenly disappeared, replaced momentarily by that commercial starring the Mud Puddle Kid.

Draped across various items of living-room furniture out there in front of the box were the three Watchers.

"That poor Kid's mother really has a problem," Number One observed, as, up on the screen, The Kid stomped gleefully through several large mud puddles. "She probably had him all ready to go to a party, and now look at him with that yucky mud all over his clothes."

"Oh, but there's Good News!" enthused Number Two excitedly. "Just watch now," he added, pointing to the screen, "and you'll see that his mom is going to

113

take all those dirty clothes and wash them in Mud-B-Gone detergent. That will solve everything!"

"If you've watched this commercial before, then you ought to know that that doesn't solve everything," retorted Number One. "Just keep watching."

They did, and sure enough, The Kid, sporting freshly laundered clothes, charged back outside to the nearest puddle. As he splattered himself with muddy goo, his mom shook her head and sighed as she tried to look thankful for her box of Mud-B-Gone.

"There, you see," Number One continued, "what good does it do for her to clean her Kid up if he goes right back out and jumps in the mud? I'll tell you what the real Good News is. It's when Mom cannot only clean The Kid up but also take away his desire to play in mud puddles—maybe even make him hate mud."

Number Three hadn't said anything so far, but he'd been thinking, and now he was ready with his dime's worth. "I think both of you may have a point," he began, "but even if Mom can clean up The Kid and then make him hate mud puddles, it seems to me that the problem can never be fully solved until someone takes the mud puddles themselves away. To me, that would really be Good News."

Well, it pains me to say it, but the three Watchers became so upset with one another over what constituted the Good News, that they stepped out into the street and started slinging mud at one another.

The last I saw them, they still hadn't figured out that they had all three seen just a part of the Good News—and that it takes all three parts to really solve The Kid's problem.

But, as Walter says, "That's the way it is."—*Insight*, February 7, 1978.

Some Christians insist that the gospel includes only

what God has done about sin's *penalty*. Others say that it also has to do with what God does about sin's *power* and *presence*—and I agree with them.

God doesn't just pardon my rebellion but leave me a rebel still. He doesn't free me from sin's penalty but leave me firmly trapped in its power. He doesn't clean me up but leave me hopelessly addicted to mud.

The Frog and the Scorpion

You've probably heard the story of the frog and the scorpion. The scorpion—who could not swim—came down to the edge of a stream one day and noticed a frog sitting there.

"Say, friend," the scorpion asked, "would you be willing to give me a ride on your back across this stream?"

"Do you take me for a fool?" the frog replied. "No sooner would I get to midstream, and you would sting me."

"Now why would I do that?" the scorpion asked. "If I stung you, we'd *both* drown."

The frog thought for a moment and decided that the scorpion made sense. So he let the scorpion climb aboard and began swimming across the stream. Halfway out, the scorpion jabbed the frog with a vicious sting.

As they both floundered in the water, the frog gasped, "You fool! Why did you do that? Now we're both going to drown."

"I know," the scorpion answered sadly as he sank beneath the surface. "But you see, I can't help it. It's just my nature."

To sin is just our nature. But the good news is not only that God has freed you from sin's penalty, but also from its power. He not only has forgiven your sin—He can keep you from sinning. The Bible says that God "is able to keep you from falling and to present you before his glorious presence without fault and with great joy." Jude 24. "No one," John wrote, "who lives in him keeps on sinning." 1 John 3:6.

And right about here, some Christians start to get nervous. They see red warning lights flashing and hear buzzers sounding. Because they have heard about a heresy called "sinless perfectionism." Is that what we're dealing with here?

Perfectionism?

Sinless perfectionism teaches that we can actually come to the place where we are so pure that sinning isn't even possible for us anymore. It teaches that getting the victory over sin is accomplished primarily by our own willpower, with an occasional assist from God. It teaches that the perfection we achieve is at least part of the basis for our acceptance by God—that our salvation depends not just on what Christ has done for us but on how sinless we become.

But the perfection—the sinlessness—the Bible talks about is something altogether different. It doesn't mean that we are incapable of sinning. It doesn't mean that we must grit our teeth and focus all our attention on ourselves in order to overcome our sins. It doesn't mean that God accepts and saves us at least partly because of how good we have become.

Unless words no longer convey their most obvious meaning, the verses we looked at above *do* say that it is possible for us to be kept from falling. They *do* say that we don't have to keep on sinning. So the Bible does clearly teach that God is fully able not only to free us from sin's penalty but also from its power.

Victory over the power of sin is not something God

requires of us in order for Him to save and accept us. It is, instead, a work that He offers to do in us if we will simply give Him the permission.

Victory over sin is not something that happens through our own effort as we anxiously monitor our own spiritual progress. It is the natural byproduct of becoming so absorbed in beholding the character of Jesus that we totally lose sight of ourselves.

And, finally, victory over sin is not to make us good enough for God to save. According to author Dick Winn, a far better reason exists: "The Christian seeks holiness of life, not so God will think better of him, but so that the world will think better of the God they see through him. The Christian detests sin in his life, not because he fears that God will think less of him, but because he fears that his friends will think less of God because of his sins."—*If God Won the War, Why Isn't It Over?* p. 44.

"Christ's love compels us," Paul wrote. "He died for all, that those who live *should no longer live for themselves but for him.*" 2 Corinthians 5:14, 15, emphasis supplied.

"Christians," Dick Winn continues, "sing, 'There is power, power, wonder-working power . . . in the precious blood of the Lamb.' And Satan taunts darkly from his corner, 'There's no power in the blood! Look at the way they live!'

"Who is telling the truth? Could you decide by doing a survey among professed Christians?

"Satan taunts Jesus with our sins. The enemy taunts the One we love! The angel promised that Jesus would save us *from* our sins. But the old snake laughs and says, 'If He saves you at all, it will have to be *in* your sins.' And some Christians slink sadly to their corners, sighing, 'Oh well, I guess forgiveness is about all I could expect, anyway.' "—*Ibid.*, pp. 45, 46.

Pardon and Power

But as electrifying as the good news is that we have been forgiven, forgiveness—pardon—is not the end of God's good news. God also offers power—power to break the chains of sinful habits, power to keep from falling, power to become like Christ.

And the purpose of this victory over sin, as the Bible says, is that we should no longer live for ourselves, but for God. We have the privilege of letting God demonstrate through us that He is able *fully* to solve the problem of sin introduced by Lucifer so long ago. That demonstration of God's power is part of the reason the great controversy did not end at the cross.

Indeed, if God won the war at the cross, why *isn't* it over? Why does the battle rage on nearly 2,000 years later? What remains to be settled before the controversy can end?

"The cross," Dick writes, "was intended for the *winning* of the controversy, but not, by itself, for the *ending* of the controversy."—*Ibid.*, p. 28.

What must happen, then, before the great controversy can end?

In the time just before Christ returns to this Earth, the Bible says, three special messages will be preached worldwide. The first of these three messages, contained in the book of Revelation, begins with these words: "Fear [worship] God and give him glory, because the hour of *his judgment* has come." Revelation 14:7, emphasis supplied.

God on Trial

The hour, the time, of God's judgment. Is it possible! God on trial! But why? Who would dare to bring charges against Him? Who indeed?

Satan, as he senses the end of the great war closing in, brings against God every charge he can think of. One of these charges that Satan has leveled against God—from the very beginning—is that God has made laws that no one can keep. Therefore, Satan says, it's no wonder he sinned—and no wonder Adam and Eve and all their descendents sinned! (This charge overlooks, of course, that at least two-thirds of the angels, who remained in Heaven, have never sinned.)

But the Bible says that when He comes back to Earth in the near future to begin the ending of the great controversy, Christ will have people on Earth who have permitted Him to keep them from falling— to deliver them from sin's power. Waiting to meet Him will be human beings who are living proof that through God's power, His laws *can* be kept—even by those who are weak and fallen. See Revelation 14:12 and Mark 4:26-29.

God will have proven that He can not only forgive sinners but change them from rebels into loyal sons and daughters once again. And He will accomplish this not by force, but by revealing the truth about Himself—truth so irresistible that human beings return to the Father's house of their own free choice.

Another reason the controversy could not end at the cross is that the world's inhabitants needed time to react to what had happened there—to absorb its meaning, to understand its significance, to be moved by its power. The cross made unmistakably clear the truth about sin, about God, and about Satan.

Choosing Up Sides

Since every one of us must ultimately choose up sides in the great controversy, God wants us to have a clear picture of what its two great opponents are really like before we decide.

And since God is fair, He wants to allow enough time not only to demonstrate the results of His love-based government of the universe, but to allow Satan to demonstrate the results of his self-based government.

God could have simply destroyed Satan and his followers when they first rebelled, but the remaining angels of Heaven—and any other inhabitants in the universe—would from then on have served God out of fear rather than love. And God does not want His created beings to serve Him from fear. So He has allowed Satan to live—and to demonstrate fully what kind of universe ours would be if this pretender were in charge.

We all know that sin brings its own brand of pleasure. But God wants to allow time enough for us to see that sin is ultimately self-destructive. He wants us to see enough of the cruel and tragic and painful and sickening results of sin that we will finally come to hate it as He does.

Yesterday, Christ suffered the *penalty* of our sins on Calvary.

Today, He offers to break the *power* of sin in our lives.

Tomorrow, He will remove even the *presence* of sin from the universe.

And, thank God, tomorrow is almost here!

Database 5, File Z-4284.900, Record 4
Journal Entry 6081.3

I doubt if anyone knows the book of lies any better than I do. I'm aware that the enemy has caused the Targets who wrote it to predict that in the end, I will lose the war. The book says I'll be destroyed. Another example of why it is, in fact, the book of lies.

I am going to win! I have the power. I have the intelligence. I have the determination. The enemy's weak and sentimental ideas about "love" as the basis for government are clearly inferior to my approach. The universe cannot function without strict discipline.

I hate him. I hate his mindless, spineless Targets. I hate his "church." I hate him—and I will destroy him. I will soon take by force what is mine, and all the universe will bow to me and to my will. I am the King. *I am the King.* I AM THE KING!

Lucifer,
Commander-in-chief, Imperial Forces
King of Earth (and soon, the Universe)
Most High God in Exile
UNIVERSAL EMPIRE

Chapter 14
The End—
The Beginning

No more will we hear from Lucifer. Because now we leave the past and present and look ahead to the future.

Against the background of a tragic cosmic war, we continue living out each day of our lives. We see evidences of the struggle all around us. We feel the force of the great tug-of-war going on over possession of our own souls. We and those we love are sometimes wounded as the battle rages on.

The days slip by. The eighties. The nineties. The dawning of a new millenium. Birthdays, holidays, graduations, weddings, funerals. Elections and Super Bowls and Olympic games. Birth, infancy, childhood, youth, middle age, retirement, old age, death. Dating, love, marriage. Babies, bottles, bills. News, sports, and weather. The New Age and the old-time religion. And finally, just God, Satan—and me.

In a blur, the days slip by. And every busy day brings The End of the war one day closer. The End. When? And how?

When? The Bible is clear that we cannot pin down the time precisely. See Matthew 24:36. But God does not want us to be totally in the dark about it, either. Many prophecies of the Bible predict the fast-closing arrival of time's final events—and we can trace their converging lines to discover that they all point to an early end to the long, expensive war.

And how? The poet T. S. Eliot wrote:

This is the way the world ends
This is the way the world ends
This is the way the world ends
Not with a bang, but a whimper

Will the world end with a nuclear bang or with the whimper of starvation? According to the Bible, just ahead of us lies a great time of trouble. See Daniel 12:1. What kind of trouble? The Bible doesn't say. But the powder keg of potential trouble is all around us. Nuclear tensions. Unstable economies. Dwindling world resources. Unpredictable terrorism. An increasingly frustrated and furious Lucifer.

The Unknown Rapture

From more and more pulpits we are told today that before the trouble comes, Jesus will "rapture" away His followers to Heaven, returning seven years later to set up an eternal kingdom on Earth. The Bible, however, knows absolutely nothing of such a teaching. But it does say that the trouble will not go on forever. Because soon, Jesus will return to Earth in indescribable splendor, surrounded by all His loyal angels, and seated on His throne as King of kings and Lord of lords.

He will not come secretly and silently—and every eye on Earth will see Him as He arrives. See Revelation 1:7 and Psalm 50:3.

As Jesus sounds a loud note on a trumpet and calls out with His voice, His followers who rest in their graves are resurrected to life again. Those we love will live again! Those of us who have chosen Jesus as our King are then lifted into the cloud surrounding Jesus, to be reunited with those who have stepped alive from their graves. See 1 Thessalonians 4:16, 17 and 1 Corinthians 15:51-55.

Those who have chosen Satan as their leader will be destroyed in the brightness of Christ's return. See 2 Thessalonians 1:7, 8 and 2:8. Those from all ages of history who have died without being reconciled to God will sleep on in their graves. See Revelation 20:5. And Satan himself will be confined to the planet Earth for the next 1,000 years. See Revelation 20:1-3.

During that 1,000 years, Christ and His followers will be in Heaven. See Revelation 20:4-6. If we are there, we will be able to review how God arrived at His decisions concerning the eternal destiny of every fallen human being and angel. See Revelation 20:4 and 1 Corinthians 6:1-3.

At the close of the 1,000 years, Jesus will return to Earth with all His redeemed followers and with the capital city of the universe—the New Jerusalem. Those of all ages who have chosen Satan as their leader will be resurrected, and Satan will be free to deceive them and stir up their hatred for Christ. See Revelation 21:2 and 20:7, 8.

The Firestorm of Hell

Satan, the Bible says, then organizes his followers to storm the city and take it by force. Will he attempt to use nuclear weapons? We don't know. What we do know is that as they prepare for the invasion, a deadly firestorm unexpectedly consumes them—and along with them, the entire face of the Earth. See Revelation 20:7-10 and 2 Peter 3:10-14.

And this fire does not, as many believe, burn

forever. The Bible is clear that it consumes the rebels of all ages, leaving nothing but ashes behind. See Malachi 4:1, 2.

Lucifer, the shining one—Lucifer, the crowning angelic creation of God—Lucifer, who once stood in his Creator's immediate presence—Lucifer, who allowed himself to be so poisoned with selfishness that he became Satan the devil—Lucifer is gone.

And I know that as God turns in disappointment from Lucifer to let him reap the final, inevitable consequences of his rebellion, He will mourn the loss of His rebel son with a grief too profound for words.

The war is over.
The great controversy is ended.
The horrible experiment with selfishness is finished.
The Lucifer Files are forever closed.

No more sin. No more suffering. No more death.

But the end is the beginning! From the ashes of a devastated world, God creates the Earth anew. He locates the capital city on the newly re-created planet—and Earth becomes the new headquarters of the universe.

God's followers, sinless, immortal, unspeakably grateful to their Creator, will have all eternity to return His love and enjoy His presence.

Only Two Choices

Yes, the war is real, my friend. And so will be the New Earth to come. As real as this book you hold in your hands. And somehow, we've just got to be there!

Only two possible destinies await us—you and me. Either we will finally reap the results of separating ourselves from God—eternal oblivion—or we will know what it is to live the first day of forever.

Two leaders to follow. Two ways of life. Two destinies. And we must choose. Those who choose not to choose will become Satan's by default. To be God's, we must choose Him deliberately, consciously.

We must choose God as our Father. We must choose God the Son—Jesus Christ—as our Creator, our Saviour, our Lord. We must choose the Holy Spirit as our Companion for all eternity. We must choose to accept whatever God offers, believe whatever He says, do whatever He asks.

We must choose soon—the war is almost over.

I see a leader consumed by rage, filled with raw hatred for me and every other living human being. I see a leader who delights in brutal cruelty and torture and pain. I see a leader filled with chilling satisfaction that he has just murdered his own Creator.

But I see another Leader. I see a Leader who loves me more than His own life—and has proven it. I see a Leader who wants nothing more than to make me happy, healthy, and holy forever. I see a Leader hanging there on a lonely cross, His heart breaking as He lets the weight of my sin crush out His life.

And the choice is instantly clear. I choose Jesus. My Leader, my Master, my Creator, my Saviour.

My Friend.